P+sitive
Alternatives to
SUSPENSION

Also from the Boys Town Press

Teaching Social Skills to Youth, 3rd Edition
Teaching Social Skills to Youth with Mental Health Disorders
Well-Managed Schools, 2nd Edition
Tools for Teaching Social Skills in School
More Tools for Teaching Social Skills in School
Everyone's Talking: Stories to Engage Middle Schoolers in Social Conversation
Take Two: Skill-Building Skits You Have Time to Do!
decoding Respect: Everyone Can Code with HTML
13 & Counting: Be the Difference!
13 & Counting: Does a Hamburger Really Have to Be Round?
13 & Counting: Rescue Me!
GRIT & Bear It! and Activity Guide
ZEST: Live It! and Activity Guide
Safe and Healthy Secondary Schools
Effective Study Strategies for Every Classroom
Working with Aggressive Youth
No Room for Bullies
No Room for Bullies: Lesson Plans for Grades 5-8
No Room for Bullies: Lesson Plans for Grades 9-12
Common Sense Parenting® DVDs:
    Building Relationships
    Teaching Children Self-Control
    Correcting Misbehavior
    Preventing Problem Behavior
    Teaching Kids to Make Good Decisions
    Helping Kids Succeed in School
Common Sense Parenting®
Common Sense Parenting® of Toddlers and Preschoolers

For Adolescents
Friend Me!
Dating!
Boundaries: A Guide for Teens
A Good Friend
Basic Social Skills for Youth

For a Boys Town Press catalog, call **1-800-282-6657**
or visit our website: **BoysTownPress.org**

Boys Town National Hotline®
1-800-448-3000
A crisis, resource and referral number for kids and parents

P+sitive
Alternatives to
SUSPENSION

❊ ❊ ❊ ❊

Procedures, Vignettes, Checklists, and Tools to Increase Teaching and Reduce Suspensions

❊ ❊ ❊ ❊

by
Catherine DeSalvo, MS
Mike Meeks, MS
Matthew Buckman, PhD

BOYS TOWN Press®

Boys Town, Nebraska

Positive Alternatives to Suspension

Published by Boys Town Press
Boys Town, NE 68010
Copyright © 2016 by Father Flanagan's Boys' Home

ISBN: 978-1-934490-99-0

Boys Town Press is the publishing division of Boys Town, a national organization serving children and families.

10 9 8 7 6 5 4 3 2

Acknowledgments

We thank the following Boys Town staff members for their contributions to the revised edition of this book and for their commitment to providing a valuable resource for all those who strive to improve the lives of children: Cedric Hunter, Sue Shupe, Erin Green, Stefanie Emrich, and Mike Sterba.

Table of Contents

SECTION 1
Introduction

The Importance of Positive Alternatives to Suspension

WE ARE TEACHERS AND TRAINERS at Boys Town, an organization dedicated to changing the way America cares for its children and families. Our part in Boys Town's mission is to help empower school personnel to proactively address the social and behavioral needs of students in ways that will help them lead successful lives.

There are numerous Boys Town publications that address a variety of ways to help students in classrooms or those who end up in the principal's office. Our approach for this book addresses the step beyond the principal's office – keeping students who have earned suspensions learning and engaged, giving them renewed hope by teaching them new pro-social skills, and keeping them up-to-date on their school work.

We are experienced in working with students in our own Boys Town middle school and high school – and in schools nationwide. We practice the Positive Alternatives to Suspension (PAS) approach and strongly believe it is an effective step to helping the most challenging students reengage behaviorally and academically.

The purpose of this book is to give school personnel tools to use to keep behaviorally challenged students in school. We will provide vignettes that you might be familiar with and introduce a process that can effect change in behavior and teach students new skills to use. School staff will be able to introduce a predictable and effective process that will link the referral behavior to alternative skills. This approach can be used in your own school even if you don't have an alternative to suspension program available to you at this time.

In talking with administrators and educators across the nation, we have heard similar stories requesting the need for an effective alternative to suspension program. They have searched for a cost-effective program that focuses on student social-emotional growth and preserves the positive culture of the school.

The goal of any school is to keep students in school, keep students and school personnel safe, and help students achieve academic and social success. In order to do this, schools must develop a system of disciplinary procedures to provide consequences for inappropriate behavior, teach pro-social skills, and remove threats to the safety of others. Unfortunately, the use of out-of-school suspension programs has limited effectiveness in simultaneously achieving all three of these goals. Some may even argue that it rewards antisocial behaviors. The overuse of out-of-school suspension has contributed to increases in student misbehavior during unsupervised days at home, loss of exposure to academic content, and school failure (American Academy of Pediatrics, 2013).

Some state legislative bodies (e.g., Connecticut) have taken the initiative to mandate the use of alternatives to suspension and limit the use of traditional out-of-school suspension. In every state, local schools have created their own version of an alternative to suspension program. This book outlines the components of and provides resources needed to implement the PAS program. The book can serve as a step-by-step guide on how to replicate an effective program that can be feasibly executed in any school to supplement an existing program or develop an alternative to out-of-school suspension.

We encourage a disciplinary system that utilizes the PAS program and out-of-school suspension strategies. The use of PAS does not mean traditional out-of-school suspension is not useful for some students. We recognize the historical benefits and current utility of using a traditional out-of-school approach to suspension. We continue to advocate for the use of traditional out-of-school suspension and expulsion for the very extreme offenders who repeatedly or significantly disrupt the school environment, elicit serious safety concerns, or refuse to participate in alternative approaches. However, it is our hope that a positive suspension experience would include the introduction of teaching social skills that would decrease the frequency, severity, and duration of student misbehavior; thus, reducing the need for more extreme disciplinary approaches.

As noted by the American Academy of Pediatrics (2013), there are generally two reasons for using traditional out-of-school suspension programs. The first is to remove potentially dangerous students from the general population to protect students and staff. The second reason is to use it as a disciplinary tactic, where a student is provided the consequence of being removed from a rewarding and positive school environment and placed into a temporarily aversive home environment. Historically, the home environment was supervised by a parent and consisted of aversive punishments, including lectures, chores, and grounding. Additionally, the student received zeros on his or her assignments and would be negatively viewed by adults and peers in the school and community. Ideally, a student would strive to avoid any repeat of this disciplinary action by working to change his or her behavior. However, this situation has changed because many parents are now unable to provide adequate supervision and consequences for their children's misbehavior at school.

Individual differences and needs should be considered when selecting an appropriate response to rule infractions. Both positive alternatives and traditional out-of-school suspension may hold a place within each school's policies and procedures. Out-of-school suspension certainly holds a place for students who threaten the safety of others and are not responsive to alternative approaches. Those who are responsive to alternative approaches like the PAS program or a permanent alternative school would be best served within these programs. The students who exhibit violent or serious behaviors may be in the most need of professional support and supervision. Their misbehavior will continue at home and in the community as long as professional supervision or assistance is not provided. Students who are not in school are likely unsupervised and will practice additional antisocial behaviors. These students may also suffer from mental health difficulties that contribute to their misbehavior which may warrant professional attention rather than expulsion from a supportive school environment.

Likewise, traditional out-of-school suspension programs treat all misbehavior as a choice by the students. These programs employ suspension as a large consequence to increase a student's motivation to use skills already known. We believe student misbehavior is the result of a lack of motivation, a performance deficit, or a skill deficit. The PAS program acknowledges the need to create structure and motivation through consequences, but there is also a need to teach students the social skills necessary to be successful in similar situations when he or she returns to the classroom.

As practitioners, we know that traditional out-of-school suspension is not implemented as it was originally intended nor does it provide the outcomes that it once did. As administrators, our purpose is to remove disruptive students in order to protect other students and the culture of the school. As disciplinarians, our purpose is to educate and provide a consequence that will reduce the likelihood of these behaviors being repeated. As educators, our purpose is to increase student academic and social success through teaching the core curriculum and social skills. As mental health professionals, our purpose is to reduce skill deficits and improve student functioning to decrease psychological suffering. Therefore, a multifaceted system for using traditional and alternative to suspension programs is needed and most effective.

The American Academy of Pediatrics (2013) recommends that...

"Out-of-school placement for suspension or expulsion should be limited to the most egregious circumstances. For in-home suspension or expulsion, the school must be able to demonstrate how attendance at the school site, even in an alternative setting with a low ratio of highly trained staff to students, would be inadequate to prevent a student from causing harm to himself or herself or to others."

School districts and health agencies all over the United States have developed programs based on this need for an alternative to out-of-school suspension. Districts have shown great creativity to address this need. Some have used in-school suspension with work completion or community service. Some have required parents to attend school with their child. Some have created skill-based programs to address student behaviors. This book highlights an effective program that addresses the goals of disciplinarians, administrators, educators, and mental health professionals.

✳ Why Do Alternatives to Suspension Work?

For a suspension experience to be worthwhile, Peterson (2005) suggests it should contain some of the following components: problem solving, contracting, making restitution, skill modules, behavior monitoring, and parental support and involvement. Many of these components can be contained in a meaningful intervention, including the Positive Alternatives to Suspension (PAS) program.

Boys Town developed its PAS program in 2009 in response to the local need for an alternative program and to address the lack of effectiveness that was reported by school administrators using traditional approaches. The core of the PAS program utilizes the decades of research and practice within the schools and the residential treatment programs at Boys Town.

One of the PAS program's primary goals is to increase student use of appropriate behaviors to achieve social and academic success while also retaining safety for all students and staff. A hallmark of the program is that it is founded on an evidenced-based approach to modifying student behavior through a respectful environment where professional support is provided and appropriate social skills are taught. For every student in the program, an individualized treatment plan is developed that involves experiential learning of social skills with a skill-based criterion for returning to school.

In one school district, the PAS program has been operating for approximately three years and has served more than two hundred students. This school has reported an overall decrease in the need for alternative and traditional suspensions since the institution of the PAS program. This program has allowed students to remain in their classrooms and has decreased the need for out-of-school or alternative suspension methods. Data collected show a twenty-three percent reduction in the total number of days suspended over a three-year trial. The number of students who earned repeat suspensions was reduced by forty-three percent over the three years. The number of suspended students verified as needing special education services was reduced by seventy-eight percent. In addition, the number of minority students suspended was reduced by forty percent. These results indicate that students benefited from the skill teaching and interventions provided by the PAS program.

Additionally, the program aims to decrease the possibility of benefits to being suspended from school and targets social skill and performance deficits for the skills needed for everyday living. Any possible benefit to being out of school during a period of suspension will be removed by keeping students in a program with high expectations and low tolerances for misbehavior. Students in the program process negative events through reflective essays that increase their understanding of the event and the consequences earned. Skills specific to the referral concerns are taught to decrease skill deficits, giving students the tools to be successful in future similar situations.

✱ Why Teach Social Skills?

The development of school behavioral problems can often be linked to students lacking the social skills needed to be successful in the school environment where they experience higher expectations and increased demands on a daily basis. These skills help students navigate their world to create and maintain relationships, overcome problems, and achieve academic and social success. According to Gresham (1998, p. 20), social skills are defined as, "…socially acceptable learned behaviors enabling the individual to interact effectively with others and avoid or escape socially unacceptable behavior exhibited by others." Thus, social skills enable students to behave appropriately and to achieve internal and external success in various environments (home, school, and work). These skills produce positive outcomes for the student and are also socially acceptable and responsive to others' needs.

Many students come from environments that have not taught or encouraged the use of appropriate social skills. Instead, these environments have taught the use of negative behaviors or inappropriate skills as ways for children to get what they need and want, and/or to avoid something they don't like or want. Although these inappropriate behaviors and skills may have been effective and produced success in one environment (home), they are viewed as unacceptable and problematic within the school environment. These inappropriate behaviors and skills are not rewarded with success in school and are often punished by teachers and peers. When these behaviors don't work, students flounder and become unsure of what it takes to be successful. Given the long history of success using negative behaviors or skills and a lack of alternative approaches, students will continue to use inappropriate skills with increased intensity and eventually disregard their desire for positive adult or peer approval. For these students to succeed in the social and academic environments, they must learn new skills to help them get their needs and wants met in socially acceptable ways that do not interfere with the academic environment. This is the aim of providing social skill instruction within the PAS program.

Students with behavior problems may have a skill or performance deficit. As was just discussed, some students may have a skill deficit because they have not been taught or mastered the social skills needed through direct instruction or appropriate modeling from close peers, adults, or both. Other students may have a performance deficit, which means a student has been taught a skill and mastered it but does not choose to display the skill when it is appropriately needed. A multitude of reasons could factor into why a student doesn't display a skill he or she has fully mastered. Some reasons proposed by Bellini (2006) include lack of motivation, sensory sensitivities, anxiety, attention problems, impulsivity, memory problems, self-efficacy deficits, and movement or motor issues.

An appropriate assessment of a student's skill versus performance deficits is needed to determine the proper approach to addressing the student's needs. Oftentimes, skill deficits and performance deficits are not exclusive. It is possible for a student to not have fully acquired a skill and to also not have the motivation to develop and use it. In these cases, both skill training and an intervention that addresses performance (e.g., motivation system, self-monitoring intervention) are necessary to target combined deficit issues.

Remediation of social skill and performance deficits should always be tailored to the individual student. Considerations for a student's developmental level, cognitive and verbal abilities, biological factors, multi-cultural background, learning history, and environmental influences should be included in the individualized plan. Each student will have a complexity of internal and environmental influences contributing to his or her social skill or performance deficits.

✳ What Is in This Book?

At the core of the PAS program is the view that behavior is something that can be taught. Teaching students socially appropriate skills can help them replace inappropriate behaviors and make better choices in school. This book offers some background on the benefits of teaching social skills to youth and procedures for setting up a PAS classroom. A checklist is also provided to assist with implementation efforts and to understand what is needed to help with the success of your program.

The book presents a series of behavioral vignettes that frequently result in suspension to guide you toward replacement skills that will likely help with recurring suspensions. The main goal of the book is to help you look at behavior objectively and look for alternative ways to teach skills to students. The recommended skills and steps are included at the back of the book and can be downloaded and printed using the included access code.

Worksheets are often helpful when a supervisor is working with more than one student. A series of writing activities can stimulate critical thinking for students. The book has samples of completed worksheets to help create criteria for student completion. However, you should avoid using the packet of materials as "busy work" and expect students to work quietly for long periods of time. Instead, the written assignments are intended to help stimulate conversation about the misbehavior and the skills needed to avoid it in the future. Some students may find writing difficult and try to avoid the task. If that is the case, you can work one-on-one with the student to help him or her get started, and use the Adaptations provided in the book and on the printable forms. The prospect of frequent positive interactions with a caring adult can improve the possibility of a student being open to practicing alternative behaviors in the future.

The PAS program is extremely effective for those students who need it. By using the suggested activities in this book and maintaining a calm, skill-focused demeanor, you and your school can help make the difficult suspension situation one that is beneficial to students and reduces the likelihood of additional suspensions.

One of the best ways to help students learn how to accept responsibility for behavior and mend relationships is to teach them how to deliver an apology. Section 4 outlines the process of doing that and provides sample resources to help students formulate an apology that includes a plan for future behavior. As a best practice, the Section 4 content should be taught to students before they the leave the PAS environment and return to the classroom. Often, students who are suspended have high anxiety about returning back to school and the classroom due to embarrassment, fear of failure, and misconceptions about school staff. Section 4 allows many of these conversations to take place in a neutral environment and helps decrease much of the student's stress. This increases the chance of a positive return to school and the classroom

Additional resources are provided in Section 5. We included this section because we know that the nine most common reasons students earn suspensions is not all-inclusive. This section contains two resources that can be used during any suspension: the SODAS and POP problem-solving methods. These can be used to help students problem solve the many possible situations they may face that have given them trouble in the past. The other forms included are focused more on additional issues that may be antecedents to student misbehavior, such as work completion and time management. You can look through this section to find skills and resources that may be appropriate for your student to learn and practice.

Included in the "Index of Skills" are the skills and specific steps for the skills identified in each chapter. PAS supervisors should use these skills and steps during role-plays with students so they can practice appropriate replacement skills. When students practice skills, they retain 70% more information than lecture alone. This best practice leads to better skill transfer and more positive behavior. What we have learned in more than 30 years of working with schools is the key to increasing positive student behavior is in the teaching that is done rather than the consequences that are given.

Implementing Best Practice for Positive Alternatives to Suspension

✳   ✳   ✳

What is Boys Town's Positive Alternatives to Suspension Program?

It is a challenge for administrators to find and develop proactive and effective ways to reach students who have serious behavior problems. Administrators know suspending students from school provides the faculty with a brief respite from repetitive disruptive behaviors, but they also know many students are likely free to sleep late, do activities they enjoy (play video games, watch TV, etc.), or get into further trouble – unless a parent is able to supervise them.

Also, there are times when student misbehavior requires a serious response that sends a message to other students, teachers, parents, board members, and the community that certain behaviors will not be tolerated and that there will be serious consequences. However, those consequences should be learning opportunities for students – after all, some good should come out of the situation. Students should benefit from a suspension experience in a practical way.

So, how can you help make this kind of positive experience happen in your school and where do you start? After you meet with the parents and student who is misbehaving, how do you provide a pertinent intervention that provides an effective consequence and does not inadvertently reinforce the behavior you are trying to decrease? It can all start with the implementation and use of the PAS program. To illustrate how this can work, let's look at the following real-life example:

Tony earned a suspension for his role in a physical altercation. While in the classroom, Tony approached another student from behind as the student was sitting at his desk and put the student's neck and head in a headlock. The student resisted and the two boys ended up in the middle of the classroom shoving and swearing at each other. Tony's teacher, Ms. Hunter, asked him to stop and calm down but Tony refused to follow her instructions, swore at her, turned over his desk, and slammed the door as he left the room. Administrators were notified of the event. The report concerned them because Tony had two other recent incidents involving seemingly unprovoked physical aggression. Tony's mother was notified and supported the decision to send Tony to PAS for two days.

This is not an uncommon occurrence in an urban middle school. What is distinctive is the administrative decision making. School administrators saw that Tony's behavior required more of a response than an afternoon in the office. In addition, Tony participates in special education services and is viewed as a student who needs individual skill instruction. In this instance, PAS is an excellent consequence to use. It allows administrators to create a structured discipline experience specifically tailored to meet Tony's needs.

What does Tony's PAS experience look like? Administrators obviously want Tony to stop fighting and bullying so he is taught social skills like following instructions, accepting criticism, getting along with peers, accepting authority, and making apologies. This allows him to learn new, non-aggressive ways to respond in the future. In addition, Tony is kept up-to-date with his classwork and given all his current assignments and the necessary assistance to complete them. Finally, Tony is provided with creative and interactive lessons on how to seek positive attention, use anger control strategies, and express feelings appropriately. This kind of two-day PAS experience provides Tony with the opportunity to further learn and hone pro-social skills while also keeping up with his academics.

An alternative to suspension like PAS helps struggling kids and their parents develop a more favorable view of the school and administrators. They see you are trying to help. Also, teachers, board members, and community members view suspension experiences as better ways to productively address behavior problems. And most importantly, students can stay at school. Most schools have the facilities and staff needed to intervene positively on behalf of these students. It just takes a plan for the intervention, a teaching format, and the understanding of what skills to teach.

✳ Schedule, Layout, Staffing, and Monitoring

Predictability is an important part of the behavior and skill-learning process. In order to make the PAS experience as predictable as possible for students, we suggest creating a schedule for what will happen while students are in PAS. Additionally, it is important to have a staff member (or interventionist) trained in the PAS program. He or she should be able to help students with both behavioral and academic issues. Often, students who earn in-school suspensions sit in a room and work on academic assignments, but they rarely get the support needed to complete the work or the behavioral re-teaching to prevent future incidents. That's why having a staff member who is able to provide assistance is so vital to the success of the PAS experience. Finally, it is important to monitor students and track their behavioral progress so you can determine if they are ready to return to the academic environment. In this chapter, we will discuss all the components necessary for making the PAS experience as effective as possible.

Schedule Considerations

A good way to show what an effective PAS schedule might look like is to provide an example. Let's look at a sample PAS schedule involving Tony, the student introduced previously. Before coming to his suspension, Tony will have likely resolved some of the immediate issues with his administrators and teachers. Tony's teachers will also have sent his assignments so he could keep up in his classes. In addition, Tony should know the reason why he earned the consequence of a suspension.

Tony's PAS schedule would include the following:

* Greeting: Staff member welcomes Tony.
* Check In: Staff member determines if Tony has the necessary materials and assignments for each class. If not, calls are made to get them. Then, the staff member can estimate the amount of time Tony needs to spend on class work, social skill work, and skill-building activities.

After the greeting and check in, the basic skills for Tony to work on during the suspension are established. Some skills that are frequently used in the suspension setting are:

* Following Instructions
* Getting the Teacher's Attention
* Staying on Task
* Ignoring Distractions by Others
* Asking Permission
* Accepting Criticism
* Making a Request

The interventionist reviews these skills with Tony and role plays them with him. The role plays can be done one-on-one with the staff member or with other students in the PAS room, and they can be done using skits or skill books. Next, Tony would write an account of the behaviors that led to the suspension. You are looking for Tony to provide an account of what happened that mirrors the teacher's report. It is important for Tony to accept responsibility for his behavior and avoid lying or blaming others.

If Tony wrote something like, "A kid really got on my nerves and I wanted to make sure he knew not to mess with me," the staff member might discuss with Tony why he felt the need to bully the student. Then, the staff member would give Tony written work that reviews and reinforces skills he can use in place of bullying and getting physical with others. Finally, the staff member would monitor, check, and intersperse this skill work with the academic work Tony brought with him.

Checklist for PAS

The following is a checklist you can use to make sure all staff and teachers involved follow a process that makes PAS predictable for students.

PAS Checklist

YES	NO	Teaching Staff
		Teachers proactively teach social skills so students can avoid future office referrals.
		When a suspension is earned, teachers send relevant academic assignments to the suspension room.
		Teachers ensure a student has a positive return to the classroom by accepting the student's apology and working to reintegrate the student by rebuilding the relationship and praising academic and behavioral successes.
YES	NO	Administration
		Teachers are notified immediately when students earn a suspension.
		Administrators periodically monitor the room and provide support as needed.
		Administrators set clear expectations for the room supervisor and any assistance regarding teaching student's social skills, monitoring behavior, and keeping data.
		Policies and procedures for managing the room are in writing and staff has copies.
		Administrators train new room supervisors and substitutes to maintain consistency.
YES	NO	Students
		Students entering the room have textbooks and materials.
		Students comply with the general code of conduct and the posted expectations.
		Students follow adults' instructions, including completing academic and skill lessons.

YES	NO	**Room Supervisor**
		Administrator informs supervisor why students are serving suspensions and for how long.
		Supervisor is encouraging and respectful to students, communicates clear expectations, is consistent, and has a low tolerance for misbehavior.
		Supervisor explains work and keeps a room log.
		Supervisor monitors and maintains an environment conducive to learning, and informs administration if additional support is required.
		Supervisor teaches social skills and is encouraging and respectful to students.
		Supervisor returns student work to appropriate teaching staff.
		Supervisor informs administration about students who do not comply with instructions.
		Supervisor collects and shares data on a daily basis and provides administration with weekly summaries.
YES	**NO**	**Room Layout**
		Desks are arranged to minimize distractions and maximize supervision and monitoring.
		Behavioral expectations are clearly posted (i.e., behavioral steps of social skills used in the curriculum) and procedures are posted.
		Academic and skill lessons are organized and materials can be retrieved quickly and easily.
YES	**NO**	**Process**
		Behavior-based placement. After students complete skill lessons, practice skills, and practice their apologies, they apologize and return to their regular classes.
		Teachers send schoolwork to the room as soon as possible, or place work in the mailbox before the school day begins. While waiting for classwork to arrive, students can work on Think Sheets, problem-solving exercises (SODAS or POP worksheets), or role plays with staff.

Room Layout Considerations

1. Locate a classroom or office area that doesn't have a lot of traffic and is isolated from the flow of the student population. The classroom should contain no more than five students in suspension at one time. You may need to look for a backup room.

2. Students will need desks or tables where they don't have to share the space and can work free from distractions. You may wish to position students facing away from each other; however, this may be unnecessary because you might have students practice skills together.

3. Each student should have access to the following:

   * Writing materials and extra paper

   * Academic assignments

   * Skills manual

   * Behavioral assignments that are contained in the skill manual

4. Arrange arrivals and departures, lunches, and bathroom breaks at times when other students aren't in the hallway.

Staff Training Considerations

When creating a successful PAS experience, one of the most important factors is staffing. The person supervising the room should be someone who:

* Has experience with students who have behavior problems and is skilled at managing behavior.

* Is willing and able to role play with students.

* Understands that social skills can be taught and learned.

* Is an independent problem solver.

* Is able to help with academic subjects or access help needed for academic work.

* Is encouraging and respectful to students.

During the suspension, students need a blend of academic and behavioral support. This allows them to learn new behaviors to replace the skill deficits that lead to the suspension, stay current with their academics, and successfully reintegrate back into the classroom.

Positive Alternatives to Suspension Rules

When a student reports for PAS, one way to insure success is to clearly pre-teach behavioral expectations. The more time spent laying out expectations and creating predictability, the fewer problems students will have with testing limits during the suspension experience. Staff members can do this through the use of Planned Teaching.

The steps to the Planned Teaching interaction are:

1. Introduce the skill.

2. Describe steps in order.

3. Give a reason.

4. Practice the skill.

The socials skills that are important to teach with Planned Teaching and to reinforce during the suspension include:

* Following Instructions

* Getting the Teacher's Attention

* Staying on Task

* Ignoring Distractions by Others

* Asking Permission

* Accepting Criticism or Consequences

* Making a Request

Monitoring Considerations

Another important part of creating predictability is behavioral tracking. Each student in PAS receives a behavior monitoring card that allows staff to track behavior and progress throughout the day. The behavior monitoring card can track both behavioral and academic assignments. The card also serves as a communication tool for teachers and parents, and provides staff with the opportunity to reinforce students for completing work. The following behavior monitoring card was adapted from *School Administrator's Resource Guide* (Boys Town Press, 2010).

Behavior Monitoring Card

STUDENT NAME:	
GRADE:	DATE:

Expectations

Follow Instructions

1. Look at the person.
2. Say "Okay" and/or nod to show understanding.
3. Do what you've been asked right away.
4. Check back (if asked).

Get Attention Appropriately

1. Look at the adult.
2. Raise your hand and stay calm.
3. Wait to be acknowledged.
4. Ask questions or make requests in a calm voice.

Stay on Task

1. Look at your task or assignment.
2. Think about the steps needed to complete the task.
3. Focus all of your attention on the task.
4. Stop working when instructed.
5. Ignore distractions and interruptions from others.

TIME	Observed Behaviors	ADULT INITIALS
8:30 - 9:00 am		
9:00 - 9:30 am		
9:30 - 10:00 am		
10:30 - 11:00 am		
11:00 - 11:30 am		
11:30 - Noon		

Noon - 12:30 pm		
12:30 - 1:00 pm		
1:30 - 2:00 pm		
2:00 - 2:30 pm		
2:30 - 3:00 pm		
3:30 - 4:00 pm		

_____   _____

SIGNATURE   DATE

Summary Report Format

After a student has completed PAS, the room supervisor or administrator will prepare a report that summarizes what the student accomplished while in PAS. This includes academic assignments completed, skills practiced, and an overall summary of the student's behavior. You can use the data from the Behavior Monitoring Card to fill out the report. Here is a blank report followed by an example with Tony.

Summary PAS Report

PERSON COMPLETING THE REPORT:
DATE ASSIGNED PAS:
Activities completed:
Skills focused on:
Overall student behaviors:

Summary PAS Report – *SAMPLE*

PERSON COMPLETING THE REPORT:	C. DeSalvo
DATE ASSIGNED PAS:	10/12/xx

Activities completed:

Tony wrote out his version of what occurred to get him sent to suspension. His account was consistent with the report that was sent from teacher.

Tony completed all math and history assignments.

Tony revised an English essay and read 30 pages in "Sounder."

Tony prepared a written and verbal apology.

Skills focused on:

Tony did work pertaining to Peer Relations and role-played and completed skill assignments. We discussed other options that he could have used. He came up with better choices other than punching his peer. He understands he could have just walked out and gotten the teacher quickly. Or if he thought his peer was going to be hurt before someone got there, he could have told the peer who was being aggressive to stop while he went to get help.

Tony wrote out a behavioral essay on fighting. He came to the conclusion that fighting doesn't solve anything. It makes you lose respect with adults as well as trust. He also said that the consequences that come along with fighting are a good deterrent for him to keep his hands to himself.

Overall student behaviors:

Tony showed remorse about his behaviors, was very receptive to feedback given to him, followed all instructions, and stayed on task.

We wish Tony success for the remainder of the school year. He seems to be a very likable young man.

Summary

To make the PAS experience effective for students and easy for staff to implement, it is important to set up the suspension environment properly. You can do this by incorporating the schedule, layout, staffing, and behavioral components discussed in this chapter. Once these are in place, your PAS program will be one that helps students and supports staff.

SECTION 3

Solutions for the Nine Most Common Reasons for Suspensions

✳   ✳   ✳

In this section, we have identified the nine most common reasons students earn suspensions. Each chapter begins with a sample scenario administrators often encounter that results in suspension. This is not an all-inclusive list of misbehaviors or scenarios; however, we have intentionally categorized them based on the most common categories identified by most education information systems, so they are generalizable to many behaviors.

After each scenario, we identify specific skills and sample resources to use when working with students in the scenarios. As an administrator or PAS supervisor, you can use these samples scenarios and resources as guidelines for working with your own students based on their individual needs. Your students may need to work on one of the behavioral-based assignments in order to learn and generalize the appropriate replacement behaviors or they may need to work on many assignments. This determination is based on the intensity, duration, and/or frequency of the incident or misbehavior that resulted in the suspension, as well as the number of times students have earned PAS.

As previously stated, it is important for students to be able to complete both academic and behavioral assignments during the PAS process. The PAS supervisor should intersperse the use of the behavioral assignments included in the following chapters with the completion of academic work, as well as take advantage of as many opportunities to debrief the assignments and discuss past and future behavioral choices. The behavioral assignments are not designed or intended to be used as "busy work" with no supervision or follow-up. Instead, they are intended to be used as conversation starters and learning tools. This makes it more likely that students will transfer skills and use them in the future.

By using these resources, you will be able to create an alternative to suspension program that is intentional about teaching replacement behaviors, while still providing an aversive consequence. In this way, students are less likely to earn additional suspensions because they have the skills necessary for future situations. And, you are creating an environment of behavioral learning rather than one built on punitive consequences and power and control. If these types of environments were successful, we wouldn't have such rampant use of suspensions.

CHAPTER 1

Code of Conduct

JIMMY HAS BEEN ASSIGNED TO THE PAS PROGRAM FOR THREE DAYS. This action was taken due to several violations of the code of conduct. Jimmy initially received an office referral from his teacher Ms. Jones for not following instructions. Ms. Jones saw that Jimmy did not complete classroom tasks in a timely manner, was talking to classmates at inappropriate times, and was struggling to accept corrective criticism by avoiding eye contact and using an argumentative tone.

Ms. Jones contacted Jimmy's mom and an after-school detention was arranged. Jimmy skipped the detention and ignored staff instructions to report to detention on the day it was assigned. This resulted in another office referral for skipping the detention. The following day, Jimmy was spotted leaving the building by staff and was directed to return to Ms. Jones' room. When he arrived, he began to argue, demanding he did not have to complete tasks assigned by Ms. Jones due to his test scores. He also argued he had already completed earlier assigned tasks. When asked to produce the completed work, he retrieved a partially completed assignment tagged with gang-style writing and graffiti. Review of other work in the class revealed other tagged assignments along with lyrics referring to guns and violence. Jimmy was referred to the office where he continued to be argumentative, disrespectful, and insubordinate. He threatened to leave without permission and was told that would result in a suspension. He continued to ignore directions and left the office. At that point, Jimmy was given the consequence of three days in the PAS program.

During PAS, Jimmy will work on the following skills:

* Accepting Criticism
* Using an Appropriate Voice Tone
* Accepting Decisions of Authority
* Doing Good Quality Work
* Showing Respect
* Following Rules

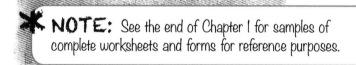

* NOTE: See the end of Chapter 1 for samples of complete worksheets and forms for reference purposes.

Avoiding Arguing

DIRECTIONS: Below are a series of statements and questions. Read them carefully and write (or check) your answers in the space provided. Use complete sentences and be prepared to discuss your answers.

Today, I argued with a...	Teacher
	Peer
	Administrator
In the past, I have...	Argued appropriately
	Argued inappropriately

There are many reasons why it is wrong to argue at school. Some of the reasons why I should not argue at school include:

- When I voice my opinion using an appropriate social skill and do not argue, others will be more willing to listen to what I have to say.
- I show respect to school staff and other students when I don't argue.
- It helps me remain calm when I express my thoughts appropriately.
- I won't interrupt or disrupt class time.
- When I am assertive rather than aggressive, people will see me as responsible and mature.
- I am likely to avoid more negative consequences when I disagree appropriately and accept consequences and decisions.
- I can avoid fights and maintain friendships.

Avoiding arguing at school is particularly important to me for two reasons (choose two from the previous list or write your own):

AVOIDING ARGUING (continued)

DIRECTIONS: Read the following information and write out your answers.

To communicate more effectively and have my thoughts and opinions taken seriously, the social skills I should use include *Accepting Criticism or a Consequence, Accepting Decisions of Authority,* and *Disagreeing Appropriately.* In the future, when I have a disagreement with a teacher or classmate, I will try to use one of these skills. The steps of the skills are:

Disagreeing Appropriately	**Accepting Decisions of Authority**	**Accepting Criticism or a Consequence**
1. Look at the person.	1. Look at the person.	1. Look at the person.
2. Use a pleasant voice tone.	2. Remain calm and monitor your feelings and behavior.	2. Say "Okay."
3. Say, "I understand how you feel."	3. Use a pleasant or neutral tone of voice.	3. Stay calm.
4. Tell why you feel differently.	4. Acknowledge the decision by saying "Okay" or "Yes, I understand."	
5. Give a reason.	5. If you disagree, do so at a later time.	
6. Listen to the other person.	6. Refrain from arguing, pouting, or becoming angry.	

In the future, I will avoid arguments by listening better, remaining calm, and talking in an appropriate voice tone. I will make sure I avoid arguments in the future by… *(describe your specific plan):*

AVOIDING ARGUING (continued)

If I need help with a skill, I will ask a teacher, counselor, or administrator to help me work on avoiding arguments or ask my family for help. **The people or resources I can use to help me are:**

At school, there are consequences for arguing with authority and others. Consequences can include correction from a teacher, detention, missed class time, meeting with a teacher or administrator, and phone calls home. In addition, there are natural consequences for arguing, including losing the respect of others, losing friendships, straining peer relationships, and losing the trust of adults and peers. **The consequences I want to avoid are:**

AVOIDING ARGUING (continued)

> **DIRECTIONS:** You may need to refer to the previous pages to answer the following questions. For each question, write a response using at least two complete sentences. If your answers are not written appropriately (capitalization, punctuation, and readable handwriting), you may have to redo the worksheet.

What are two reasons why arguing makes it harder for others to listen to you?

1.

2.

How does arguing at school hurt you?

What two actions or steps do you plan to take to avoid arguing with others at school?

1.

2.

**There may be more negative consequences in the future if you argue at school.
What are two possible consequences?**

What are two benefits or good things that can happen when you share your thoughts appropriately without arguing?

1.

2.

_____   _____
SIGNATURE   DATE

Accepting the Decisions of Authority

DIRECTIONS: Read the following sentences carefully and answer by filling in the blanks or writing in the space provided. Please use complete sentences.

I did not accept the decision of an authority figure when I...
(describe the situation, including who was involved and your behavior):

The reasons why I did not accept the decision were:

List three ways you can avoid this problem in the future, then circle the best one:

1.

2.

3.

Accepting the Decisions of Authority

DIRECTIONS: Read the following paragraphs and be prepared to have a discussion with your teacher/administrator.

Accepting the decisions of authority figures (teachers, coaches, and administrators) is a rule and a skill I need to learn in order to be successful in and outside of school. When I refuse to accept their decisions by arguing, acting out, or making threats, I am not meeting the school's social and behavioral expectations. I make it difficult for the class or school to run smoothly, and I often make things more difficult for me and the people around me.

If I do not follow the decisions of authority figures, I can put myself and others in unsafe situations. I also set a bad example for my peers because I am showing disrespect and acting childish. I understand that although I may not like every decision that is made, there is an appropriate time, place, and way to disagree. I did not disagree appropriately. I also understand that part of growing up is understanding even when I disagree appropriately, sometimes authority figures may make a decision for the good of everyone I do not agree with. Sometimes, these decisions may even make things more difficult for me. I understand I may not have enough information or experience to know what is best.

However, when I do accept the decisions of authority figures, I help my class and school run smoothly and show respect to others. I also avoid earning unnecessary negative consequences.

When I'm older, the consequences can be more serious if I do not follow the decisions of authority figures. On the job, when employees argue with their bosses, they are viewed as difficult employees. They can lose out on promotions or lose their jobs. **However, employees who do meet the expectations of their bosses are valued and sometimes promoted.**

I understand my teacher is trying to help me learn how to accept decisions made by authority figures so I will have more success at school and in the future. It is my responsibility to fix this behavior. If I do not use the skill of **Accepting Decisions of Authority,** I will earn additional consequences.

I will strive to do better in the future.

_____   _____
SIGNATURE   DATE

Accepting Criticism

DIRECTIONS: Sit quietly and answer the following essay questions on a separate sheet of paper. Print or write neatly. When finished, raise your hand and be prepared to discuss the essay.

What did I do wrong?

What could happen to me?

Why was it wrong?

What should I do?

What good things will happen to me?

Avoiding Arguing

DIRECTIONS: Below are a series of statements and questions. Read them carefully and write (or check) your answers in the space provided. Use complete sentences and be prepared to discuss your answers.

Today, I argued with a...	X	Teacher
		Peer
		Administrator
In the past, I have...	X	Argued appropriately
		Argued inappropriately

There are many reasons why it is wrong to argue at school. Some of the reasons why I should not argue at school include:

- When I voice my opinion using an appropriate social skill and do not argue, others will be more willing to listen to what I have to say.
- I show respect to school staff and other students when I don't argue.
- It helps me remain calm when I express my thoughts appropriately.
- I won't interrupt or disrupt class time.
- When I am assertive rather than aggressive, people will see me as responsible and mature.
- I am likely to avoid more negative consequences when I disagree appropriately and accept consequences and decisions.
- I can avoid fights and maintain friendships.

Avoiding arguing at school is particularly important to me for two reasons (choose two from the previous list or write your own):

I show respect to school staff and other students when I don't argue.

I am likely to avoid more negative consequences when I disagree appropriately and accept consequences and decisions.

AVOIDING ARGUING (continued)

DIRECTIONS: Read the following information and write out your answers.

To communicate more effectively and have my thoughts and opinions taken seriously, the social skills I should use include *Accepting Criticism or a Consequence, Accepting Decisions of Authority,* and *Disagreeing Appropriately.* In the future, when I have a disagreement with a teacher or classmate, I will try to use one of these skills. The steps of the skills are:

Disagreeing Appropriately	Accepting Decisions of Authority	Accepting Criticism or a Consequence
1. Look at the person.	1. Look at the person.	1. Look at the person.
2. Use a pleasant voice tone.	2. Remain calm and monitor your feelings and behavior.	2. Say "Okay."
3. Say, "I understand how you feel."	3. Use a pleasant or neutral tone of voice.	3. Stay Calm.
4. Tell why you feel differently.	4. Acknowledge the decision by saying "Okay" or "Yes, I understand."	
5. Give a reason.	5. If you disagree, do so at a later time.	
6. Listen to the other person.	6. Refrain from arguing, pouting, or becoming angry.	

In the future, I will avoid arguments by listening better, remaining calm, and talking in an appropriate voice tone. I will make sure I avoid arguments in the future by... *(describe your specific plan):*

When my teacher comes to talk to me, I will look at her right away and listen when she is talking.

42

AVOIDING ARGUING (continued)

If I need help with a skill, I will ask a teacher, counselor, or administrator to help me work on avoiding arguments or ask my family for help. **The people or resources I can use to help me are:**

If I need help, I can ask Mr. McLeod to practice with me.

At school, there are consequences for arguing with authority and others. Consequences can include correction from a teacher, detention, missed class time, meeting with a teacher or administrator, and phone calls home. In addition, there are natural consequences for arguing, including losing the respect of others, losing friendships, straining peer relationships, and losing the trust of adults and peers. **The consequences I want to avoid are:**

My mom and dad being mad at me and my teacher being mad at me all the time.

AVOIDING ARGUING (continued)

DIRECTIONS: You may need to refer to the previous pages to answer the following questions. For each question, write a response using at least two complete sentences. If your answers are not written appropriately (capitalization, punctuation, and readable handwriting), you may have to redo the worksheet.

What are two reasons why arguing makes it harder for others to listen to you?

1. When I argue it is difficult for me to hear what the other person is saying, and they may not want to listen.

2. When I argue, sometimes I yell and that makes other people not want to listen.

How does arguing at school hurt you?

Arguing with teachers gets you in trouble.

When you are always arguing, teachers may not want to help you.

What two actions or steps do you plan to take to avoid arguing with others at school?

1. I will look at the teacher and say okay when they are talking.

2. I will also listen to the teacher's feedback and if I have concerns, I will talk to the teacher later.

AVOIDING ARGUING (continued)

There may be more negative consequences in the future if you argue at school. What are two possible consequences?

One consequence is that I will get a reputation of being a smart aleck, and people won't want to help me.

Another consequence is I will get into trouble with my mom at home.

What are two benefits or good things that can happen when you share your thoughts appropriately without arguing?

1. If I can share my thoughts and ideas calmly, my ideas will be accepted.

2. I will have more people who want to help me if I listen and don't argue.

Jimmy Jackson

8/24/xx

SIGNATURE

DATE

Accepting the Decisions of Authority

DIRECTIONS: Read the following sentences carefully and answer by filling in the blanks or writing in the space provided. Please use complete sentences.

I did not accept the decision of an authority figure when I…
(describe the situation, including who was involved and your behavior):

I argued with Mr. Frost over a math assignment. I yelled, swore, and tore up the assignment.

The reasons why I did not accept the decision were:

I was mad because I did half the assignment. He should have given me some credit.

List three ways you can avoid this problem in the future, then circle the best one:

1.   I can take better notes in class.

2.   I can complete the whole assignment next time.

3.   I can listen more calmly the next time he gives me instructions on the assignment.

Accepting Criticism

DIRECTIONS: Sit quietly and copy the following essay questions and answers on a separate sheet of paper. Print or write neatly. When finished, raise your hand and be prepared to discuss the essay.

What did I do wrong?

I did not accept criticism. I made a poor choice, and now I have to copy this essay. I should have accepted the criticism I was given by looking at the person and saying, "Okay." That's how I should accept criticism.

What could happen to me?

When I don't accept criticism, I can earn more negative consequences, including spending time in the office, detention, or suspension. I will have to write, practice, and deliver an apology to the person whose criticism I did not accept. There will be a phone call home, too. If I continue to make poor choices by not accepting criticism, the consequences will get larger and more severe.

Why was it wrong?

I know that not accepting criticism is a poor choice. It shows that I am not very mature and am unable to listen to information people are trying to give me. I will bring more negative attention to myself, and other students might think I have problems. When I don't accept criticism, someone has to show me how to make a better choice.

INTERVENTIONIST TIP:
Good tool to use with non-workers or students who require additional support.

ACCEPTING CRITICISM (continued)

What should I do?

From now on, I will accept criticism by looking at the person and saying, "Okay." I will accept the criticism I'm given, even when I don't agree, because that is the best choice I can make. I will tell myself, "I am going to accept criticism, and I'm going to do a good job at it." When I accept criticism, I won't get in trouble, and I won't have to copy this essay again.

What good things will happen to me?

I know that if I can accept criticism, good things will happen to me. I will learn what I'm doing wrong so I won't repeat the same mistakes. I will show others I am more mature because I'm willing to change and make improvements. Most importantly, I will show respect to my teachers and classmates, which will improve my relationships with them.

Defiance, Non-Compliance, and Insubordination

MARK HAS BEEN REFERRED TO THE OFFICE BY MRS. SMITH FOR DEFIANCE. The referral report states that Mrs. Smith asked Mark to stop talking to his friend Eric during a math lecture. Mark continued to talk and ignored Mrs. Smith's direction. She prompted Mark to stop talking again and Mark yelled, "Hold on! I'm almost finished!" She walked over to Mark to continue the conversation and he said, "Why are you coming over here? This is none of your business!" The other students started laughing, and Mark got up from his desk and left the classroom to go to the bathroom without asking permission. Mrs. Smith sent Mark to the office for being defiant, talking out, and leaving the classroom without asking permission. This is Mark's third office referral this week for defiant behavior in the classroom and he earned a one-day suspension as a consequence.

During PAS, Mark will work on the following skills:

* Following Instructions
* Asking Permission
* Following Rules
* Complying with Reasonable Requests
* Accepting Decisions of Authority
* Disagreeing Appropriately
* Accepting Criticism

Defiance, Non-Compliance, and Insubordination

Following Instructions

DIRECTIONS: Below are a series of statements and questions. Read them carefully and write (or check) your answers in the space provided. Use complete sentences and be prepared to discuss your answers.

Today, I argued with a...	Teacher
	Peer
	Administrator
In the past, I have...	Followed instructions
	Not followed instructions

I am expected to follow instructions at school because it is a school and classroom rule. Today, I did not follow the instructions of (write person's name):

There are many reasons why it is important to follow instructions. Some of the reasons why I should follow instructions at school include:

- I am more likely to do better on assignments and projects, which may improve my grades.
- By following instructions, I will be able to do things correctly the first time.
- I may have less homework because I don't have to redo assignments.
- I show respect to my teachers and peers by helping the class run more smoothly.
- I show teachers I'm responsible because they don't always have to correct or prompt me.
- I can make following instructions a habit, which will help me in the future.
- I avoid being corrected by my teachers and earning negative consequences.

Following instructions is particularly important to me for two reasons
(choose two from the previous list or write your own):

FOLLOWING INSTRUCTIONS (continued)

In the future, I will try to follow instructions by correctly using the skill of **Following Instructions.** The steps of the skill are:

- **Look at the person.**
- **Say "Okay."**
- **Ask for clarification if needed.**
- **Do what you have been asked right away.**
- **Check back if that is part of the instruction.**

In the future, I will make sure I follow instructions by...
(describe your specific plan and identify the skill steps you need to improve on the most):

If I need help with this skill, I will ask a teacher or administrator to help me work on following instructions. Or, I will talk to a friend or family member about the skill. **The people or resources I can use to help me are:**

At school, there are consequences for not following instructions. Consequences can include correction from a teacher, loss of a privilege or activity, detention, office referral, meeting with a teacher or administrator, and phone calls home. In addition, there are natural consequences for not following instructions, including falling behind in homework, earning lower grades, having less time to spend with friends, and feeling embarrassed. **The consequences I want to avoid are:**

FOLLOWING INSTRUCTIONS (continued)

DIRECTIONS: You may need to refer to the previous pages to answer the following questions. For each question, write a response using at least two complete sentences. If your answers are not written appropriately (capitalization, punctuation, and readable handwriting), you may have to redo the worksheet.

What are two reasons why it's important to follow instructions at school and school-sponsored events?

How does not following instructions affect school performance?

What are actions or steps you can take that can help you with following instructions at school?

There may be more negative consequences in the future for not following instructions. What are two possible consequences?

What are two benefits or good things that can happen when instructions are followed?

SIGNATURE

DATE

Following Instructions/Procedures

DIRECTIONS: Sit quietly and answer the following essay questions on a separate sheet of paper. Print or write neatly. When finished, raise your hand and be prepared to discuss the essay.

What did I do wrong?

What could happen to me?

Why was it wrong?

What should I do?

What good things will happen to me?

Following Instructions/Procedures

DIRECTIONS: Sit quietly and copy the following essay questions and answers on a separate sheet of paper. Print or write neatly. When finished, raise your hand and be prepared to discuss the essay.

What did I do wrong?

Today, I was sent out of the classroom/lab because I did not follow the instructions/ procedures. I made a poor choice, and now I have to copy this essay. My teacher has a procedure for working in the classroom/lab, and I did not follow those instructions. I did not use the classroom/lab materials in a safe manner.

What could happen to me?

When I don't follow instructions/procedures, I disrupt others and create a situation that is unsafe. I can earn more negative consequences, including spending time in the office, in detention, or in suspension. I will have to write, practice, and deliver an apology to my teacher. There will be a phone call home, too. If I continue to make poor choices by not following instructions/procedures, the consequences will get larger and more severe.

Why was it wrong?

I know that not following instructions/procedures is a poor choice. It shows that I am not very mature, and I am being disrespectful to my teacher and classmates. My actions put me and others at risk. When I don't follow instructions/procedures, someone has to show me how to make a better choice.

What should I do?

From now on, I will follow instructions/procedures by doing what I have been asked and staying on task. I will tell myself, "I am going to follow instructions and procedures so class is more fun and safe for me."

What good things will happen to me?

I know that if I can follow instructions/procedures, good things will happen to me. When I follow instructions/procedures, I stay out of trouble, help keep the classroom/lab safe, and I won't have to copy this essay again. I will show others I am mature and responsible.

Asking Permission and Following Rules

DIRECTIONS: Read the following information and write out your answers.

In the future, I will use the skills of *Asking Permission* and *Following Rules.*
The steps of the skills are:

Asking Permission	**Following Rules**
1. Look at the person.	1. Learn what rules apply to the current situation.
2. Use a calm and pleasant voice.	2. Adjust your behavior so that you are following those rules exactly.
3. Say "May I...?"	3. Don't "bend" rules, even just a little.
4. Accept the answer calmly.	4. If you have questions, find the appropriate adult to ask about the rules in question.

In the future, if I do not have permission to leave, I will stay in my assigned location.
If I feel frustrated or am told I cannot leave, I will use a calming strategy (positive self-talk, silently counting to ten, or deep breathing). I understand that I will not always be given permission to leave, and I will have to remain calm by using my self-control plan. I will make sure I always ask permission first and respond appropriately if the answer is "No" by... *(describe your specific plan):*

If I need help with a skill, I will ask a teacher, counselor, or administrator to help me or ask my family for help. This shows responsibility, which is an important character trait.
The people or resources I can use to help me are:

ASKING PERMISSION AND FOLLOWING RULES (continued)

Between Asking Permission and Following Rules, the skill I need the most help with is:

The steps of the skill are:

At school, there are consequences for leaving without permission. Consequences can include an automatic office referral, detention, mediation time, phone calls to police or home, in-school suspension, and out-of-school suspension. In addition, there are natural consequences for leaving without permission, including missing schoolwork, falling behind, losing the respect of others, and losing the trust of adults and peers. **The consequences I want to avoid are:**

ASKING PERMISSION AND FOLLOWING RULES (continued)

> **DIRECTIONS:** You may need to refer to the previous pages to answer the following questions. For each question, write a response using at least two complete sentences. If your answers are not written appropriately (capitalization, punctuation, and readable handwriting), you may have to redo the worksheet.

What are two reasons why it is important to never leave school or class without permission?

How does leaving class or school without permission affect your school day?

What are two actions or steps that you can take to remember to ask permission to leave class?

There may be more consequences in the future for leaving without permission. What are two possible consequences?

What are two benefits or good things that can happen you stay in class or school until dismissed?

_____   _____

SIGNATURE   DATE

CHAPTER 3

Harassment/ Boundaries

JACK WAS REFERRED TO **PAS** DUE TO EXPLICIT SEXUAL COMMENTS HE MADE ABOUT SALLY'S BODY PARTS. Sally had asked Jack on three occasions to stop making sexual comments but he just laughed and continued to make loud remarks about her "butt." Later, a faculty member observed Jack grab Sally's bottom and he was referred to the office. While in the office, Jack refused to take responsibility for his comments and actions and was dishonest by denying what he said and did. Because Jack has been to the office on other occasions for similar inappropriate behaviors with female peers, he earned a two-day referral to the PAS program.

During PAS, Jack will work on the following skills:

* Choosing Appropriate Words to Say
* Controlling Emotions
* Making a Request

* Accepting "No"
* Dealing with Frustration
* Using Appropriate Voice Tone
* Following Instructions
* Accepting Criticism
* Greeting Others
* Self-Correcting Own Behavior
* Problem-Solving a Disagreement
* Compromising with Others
* Making an Apology

Choosing Appropriate Words to Say

DIRECTIONS: Below are a series of statements and questions. Read them carefully and write (or check) your answers in the space provided. Use complete sentences and be prepared to discuss your answers.

I am expected to interact appropriately with peers at school because it is a school and classroom rule. **Today, I did not interact appropriately with…**
(write person's name):

In the past, I have…	Chosen appropriate words to say
	Not chosen appropriate words to say

There are many reasons why it is important to **choose appropriate words to say.** Some of the reasons why I should interact appropriately with others at school include:

- I am more likely have more friends.
- By observing personal boundaries, I will develop positive peer relationships.
- I show respect to my peers by helping make sure everyone feels safe around me.
- I show teachers I'm responsible because they don't have to watch my every move.
- I can make respecting others' boundaries a habit, which will help me in the future.
- I avoid being corrected by my teachers and earning negative consequences.

Choosing appropriate words to say is particularly important to me for two reasons (choose two from previous the list or write your own):

CHOOSING APPROPRIATE WORDS TO SAY (continued)

In the future, I will correctly use the skill of **Choosing Appropriate Words to Say**. The steps of the skill are:

- Look at the situation and the people around you.

- Know the meanings of words you are about to say.

- Refrain from using words that will offend people around you or that they will not understand.

- Avoid using slang, profanity, or words that could have a sexual meaning.

- Decide what thought you want to put into words and then say the words.

In the future, I will make sure to **choose appropriate words to say** by…
(describe your specific plan and identify the skill steps you need to improve on the most):

If I need help with this skill, I will ask a teacher or administrator to help me work on **choosing appropriate words to say**. Or, I will talk to a friend or family member about the skill. **The people or resources I can use to help me are:**

At school, there are consequences for not interacting appropriately with peers. Consequences can include correction from a teacher, loss of a privilege or activity, detention, office referral, meeting with a teacher or administrator, and phone calls home. In addition, there are natural consequences, including getting caught by teachers, other students avoiding me, people getting angry at me and feeling embarrassed. **The consequences I want to avoid are:**

CHOOSING APPROPRIATE WORDS TO SAY (continued)

> **DIRECTIONS:** You may need to refer to the previous pages to answer the following questions. For each question, write a response using at least two complete sentences. If your answers are not written appropriately (capitalization, punctuation, and readable handwriting), you may have to redo the worksheet.

What are two reasons why it's important to choose appropriate words to say in class and school-sponsored events?

How does not interacting appropriately with others affect your school day?

What are two actions or steps that can be taken to help with choosing appropriate words to say?

There may be more negative consequences in the future when not interacting appropriately with others. What are two possible consequences?

What are two benefits or good things that can happen when interacting appropriate with others?

_____
SIGNATURE

_____
DATE

Choosing Appropriate Words to Say

DIRECTIONS: Sit quietly and answer the following essay questions on a separate sheet of paper. Print or write neatly. When finished, raise your hand and be prepared to discuss the essay.

What did I do wrong?

What could happen to me?

Why was it wrong?

What should I do?

What good things will happen to me?

CHAPTER 4

Fighting

DAVID WAS REFERRED TO THE **PAS** PROGRAM DUE TO REPEATED PEER RELATIONS DIFFICULTIES. In the past three months, David has been referred to the office six times regarding conflict with peers. He has been in two physical altercations and four verbally aggressive fights with peers following disagreements. The current referral pertains to an incident that occurred at lunch. David told one of his peers to let him copy his homework. The student told David he would not let him cheat. David became angry and insisted the peer share his homework. David then tried to take the homework out of the peer's backpack and the student grabbed David's arm. David pushed the student to the ground and pushed him again when he tried to get up. David then began crying and yelled, "I just wanted the homework! I thought you were my friend!" At this time, Mr. Smith intervened and took both students to the office. Due to David's past peer conflicts, he was assigned to PAS. Staff met with David's father who reported David frequently talks about peers being mean to him. David was told that PAS will be an opportunity for him to learn some skills to help him the next time this happens.

During PAS, the skills David will work on are:

* Cooperating with Others
* Coping with Anger and Aggression from Others* (*If it is determined you have been the victim of aggression)
* Coping with Conflict
* Compromising with Others
* Accepting "No"
* Communicating Honestly
* Analyzing Tasks to be Completed
* Controlling Emotions

Avoiding Fighting

DIRECTIONS: Sit quietly and answer the following essay questions on a separate sheet of paper. Print or write neatly. When finished, raise your hand and be prepared to discuss the essay.

Why do people fight?

What does fighting solve?

What happens when you fight?

How can you avoid fights?

Avoiding Fighting

DIRECTIONS: Sit quietly and copy the following essay questions and answers on a separate sheet of paper. Print or write neatly. When finished, raise your hand and be prepared to discuss the essay.

Why do people fight?

Sometimes people fight when they can't get their way. Some people fight when they can't win an argument. Some people fight just to bully people. Some people fight to protect themselves from bullies. Some people fight because they cannot handle feeling angry or frustrated. There are many reasons why people fight, but whenever you get into a fight, you get into trouble.

What does fighting solve?

Fighting never made anybody stronger, more intelligent, or cooler. Fighting is stupid. It may seem as if it solves problems for a while, but in the long run it just causes more problems. The problem that caused the fight is still there, plus you are in more trouble for fighting. If people don't like you, fighting them isn't going to make them like you more. Besides, people usually get hurt in fights and sometimes it can be really serious.

What happens when you fight?

When you fight, people don't want to hang out around you because you fight. People don't want to be around people who fight. People who fight are called bullies and trouble makers. I got into a fight, and now I have to copy this essay.

How can you avoid fights?

1. Don't start fights.

2. Don't hang around people who fight.

3. Don't let others start fights with you.

4. Remember what happens when you fight.

Avoiding Fighting

DIRECTIONS: Read the following information and write out your answers.

1. **What did you do to get into trouble?**

    _____

    _____

    _____

    _____

2. **How did you and other people get hurt by this situation?**

    _____

    _____

    _____

    _____

3. **Why did you do it?** *(Circle all that apply)*
    *   Everyone does it
    *   Some people deserve it
    *   It can be fun
    *   It makes me popular
    *   Others expect me to be aggressive or bully
    *   It makes me feel better
    *   People notice me more when I bully
    *   I am bullied so why not bully other people too?

AVOIDING FIGHTING (continued)

4. Everyone does it

Would you follow the crowd by choosing to hurt others? Although sometimes it feels like everyone fights, only a small number of students get into fights. Usually kids try to get others to fight but aren't around when you get into trouble, and they would never want to get caught fighting.

What will happen if you don't follow the crowd?

Good Outcomes: _____

_____

_____

_____

_____

Bad Outcomes: _____

_____

_____

_____

_____

_____

5. They deserved it

Why do you think some people deserve to be hurt? Sometimes, students are not good at getting along with others or annoy others with the way they talk or habits they have. Other times, they may try to make you angry to get you into trouble.

Do you deserve to be hurt for things you do? _____

_____

_____

_____

AVOIDING FIGHTING (continued)

6. It can be fun

Sometimes students feel strong when they fight. Sometimes they would rather get into trouble than to feel weak. Controlling our anger and feeling good about ourselves without fighting is another way of being strong.

Why is fighting fun for you? _____

_____

_____

Do you remember a time when it wasn't fun? _____

_____

_____

Do you think it is fun for the person being hurt? Explain why. _____

_____

_____

7. It makes me popular

When students fight they become less popular with some and more popular with others.

What friends would you lose if you chose not to fight? _____

_____

_____

8. Others expect me to fight

Sometimes students who are your friends can pressure you to do something you are uncomfortable with or you may get in trouble for doing.

How do your friends pressure you to fight? _____

_____

_____

_____

AVOIDING FIGHTING (continued)

What would happen if you chose not to fight? _____

_____

_____

_____

What could you say or do when you decide not to fight? _____

_____

_____

_____

What friends like you for who you are and don't pressure you to fight?_____

_____

_____

_____

9.   It makes me feel better

Some students report fighting makes them feel better; however, getting in trouble or losing privileges doesn't feel good. Planning alternative ways of feeling good rather than being aggressive or fighting may increase your success in the future.

If you had other ways of feeling good would you use them? Why would you use them? _____

_____

_____

_____

_____

What are some things you could do to relieve unpleasant feelings or create happiness other than fighting? (Examples: take a walk, exercise, listen to music, count to 10 or 100, talk with a friend, tell a teacher.)

_____

_____

_____

_____

AVOIDING FIGHTING (continued)

10. People notice me more when I am aggressive or fight

Sometimes students get more attention for fighting. They get respect from others who fight and are feared by others.

How does fighting bring you attention from others? _____

_____

_____

What ways could you be noticed without fighting? _____

_____

_____

11. I get really angry

Sometimes anger can get students into trouble. Knowing and practicing calming responses when angry can help.

In what ways can you calm yourself when frustrated, upset, or angry? _____

_____

What can you do to not get into fights in the future? _____

_____

_____

Who can you talk with for help or support if a conflict arises? Name/Relationship? _____

_____

_____

12. What have I learned?

Part of growing from an experience is to recognize how to make better choices in the future.

Write about the alternatives you have to getting into fights and why they are good alternatives.

_____

_____

CHAPTER 5

Bullying/ Threatening Others

WHILE AT LUNCH, JASON GREW ANGRY WITH A FEMALE STUDENT (JENNIFER) BECAUSE SHE WAS SITTING IN "HIS SEAT," referring to the table and place he normally sits at during lunch. However, Jason didn't have an assigned seat so it was first-come-first-served seating. After the girl refused to move, Jason said, "B---h! I am going to bring a gun tomorrow and shoot your a--!" He repeated it to her a second time and sat down at a nearby table while glaring at her. Jason has been observed intimidating this same student on several occasions. He presents by posturing towards Jennifer and others and making threats to intimidate them. A risk assessment was conducted and Jason did not have access to any weapons and had no intentions to follow through with his threat. He reported, "I was just joking. She knows not to sit in my seat." Staff met with Jason's grandmother and the family was very supportive.

During PAS, Jason will work on these skills:

* Controlling Emotions
* Making a Request
* Accepting "No"
* Dealing with Frustration
* Using Anger Control Strategies
* Using Appropriate Voice Tone
* Following Instructions
* Accepting Criticism
* Greeting Others
* Self-Correcting Own Behavior
* Showing Respect
* Problem Solving a Disagreement
* Compromising with Others
* Making an Apology

✳ Types of Bullying

The following are definitions of the different types of bullying:

PHYSICAL BULLYING
Includes threatening someone with physical violence or harm such as kicking, hitting, punching, pulling, or touching inappropriately. Physical bullying also includes taking or destroying property.

VERBAL BULLYING
Includes calling people bad names, teasing, taunting, making offensive remarks, criticizing them or the way they look, gossiping, or making fun of them.

SOCIAL BULLYING

Includes excluding others from group activities, spreading rumors or stories about them, telling others something said in private, gossiping, taunting, giving someone the silent treatment, or making friendship conditional.

CYBER BULLYING

Includes the use of electronic media – computers, cell phones, texting, sexting, cameras, etc. – to send negative messages, pictures, and information to other people without their permission. Cyber bullies often don't recognize it as something wrong.

Positive Alternatives to Suspension

Refraining from Bullying Others

DIRECTIONS: Read the questions and write out your answers.

1. What bullying did you do?

_____

_____

_____

_____

2. How did the person respond? How do you think the person felt?

_____

_____

_____

_____

3. Why did you bully? *(Circle all that apply)*

- Everyone does it
- Some people deserve it
- It can be fun
- It makes me popular
- Others expect me to be aggressive or bully
- It makes me feel better
- People notice me more when I bully
- I am bullied so why not bully other people too?

REFRAINING FROM BULLYING OTHERS (continued)

4. Everyone does it

Although it might feel like everyone bullies at times, only a small number of students bully and many only do it because they think others want them to do it.

Would you follow the crowd by choosing to hurt others? _____

_____

_____

What will happen if you don't follow the crowd?

Good Outcomes: _____

_____

Bad Outcomes: _____

_____

5. They deserved it

Why do you think some people deserve to be bullied or hurt? Sometimes, students are not good at getting along with others or annoy others with the way they talk or habits they have. Other times, they may try to make you angry to get you into trouble.

Why do you think some people deserve to be bullied? _____

_____

_____

Do you deserve to be bullied? _____

_____

_____

REFRAINING FROM BULLYING OTHERS (continued)

6. It can be fun

Some bullies report that it feels good to have power or control. If we use our strengths, we find we are powerful and have control in other ways instead of bullying.

Why is bullying fun? _____

_____

_____

Do you remember a time when it wasn't fun? _____

_____

_____

Do you think it is fun for the person being hurt? Explain why. _____

_____

_____

7. It makes me popular

When students bully they become less popular with some and more popular with others.

What friends would you lose if you weren't aggressive or a bully? _____

_____

_____

What friends would you be less popular with because you are aggressive or a bully? _____

_____

_____

8. Others expect me to be a bully or aggressive

Sometimes, students who are your friends can pressure you to do something you are uncomfortable with or you may get in trouble for doing.

How do your friends pressure you to be aggressive or bully others? _____

_____

_____

REFRAINING FROM BULLYING OTHERS (continued)

What would happen if you chose not to be aggressive or bully others? _____

_____

_____

What could you say or do when you decide not to bully others? _____

_____

_____

9. It makes me feel better

Some students report that bullying or being aggressive makes them feel better; however, getting in trouble or losing privileges doesn't feel good. Planning alternative ways of feeling good rather than being aggressive or bullying may increase your success in the future.

If you had other ways of feeling good would you use them? Why would you use them? _____

_____

_____

_____

What are some things you could do to relieve unpleasant feelings or create happiness other than bullying? (For example: take a walk, exercise, listen to music, count to 10 or 100, talk with a friend, tell a teacher.)_____

_____

_____

10. People notice me more when I am aggressive

Sometimes, students get more attention for bullying. They get support from other bullies and attention from the fear felt by others.

How does bullying bring you attention from others?_____

_____

_____

_____

REFRAINING FROM BULLYING OTHERS (continued)

What ways could you get noticed without being aggressive or bullying? _____

_____

_____

11. I am bullied so why not bully other people too?

Some bullies are also bullied by others and think it's normal. It is not. It can be stopped.

How does bullying others diminish your chances of being bullied? _____

_____

_____

How does it feel to be bullied by others? _____

_____

_____

How do you think the people you are bullying feel? _____

_____

_____

12. What have I learned?

As you reflect on what you have learned about your past behavior regarding bullying, write about why you think you have been a bully towards others. _____

_____

_____

_____

Part of growing from an experience is to recognize how to make better choices in the future. Write about what alternatives you have to bullying and why they are good alternatives. _____

_____

_____

_____

Controlling Emotions

DIRECTIONS: Sit quietly and answer the following essay questions on a separate sheet of paper. Print or write neatly. When finished, raise your hand and be prepared to discuss the essay.

What did I do wrong?

What could happen to me?

Why was it wrong?

What should I do?

What good things will happen to me?

Controlling Emotions

DIRECTIONS: Sit quietly and copy the following essay questions and answers on a separate sheet of paper. Print or write neatly. When finished, raise your hand and be prepared to discuss the essay.

What did I do wrong?

I am serving an in-school suspension because I did not control my emotions or my behaviors. I made poor choices, and now I have to copy this essay. I also know I will have to make up assignments and other school work because I am serving a suspension.

What could happen to me?

When I don't control my emotions, I disrupt others and create situations that are unsafe. I set a poor example for my peers. I also earn negative consequences, including office referrals, detentions, and in-school suspensions. I will have to write, practice, and deliver an apology to my teacher. There will be a phone call home, too. If I continue to make poor choices by not controlling my emotions, the consequences will get more severe.

Why was it wrong?

When I can't control my emotions, especially when I am angry or frustrated, I disrupt everyone around me. I make it harder for my classmates to stay on task, and I make it harder for my teachers and others. My poor choices are a sign of disrespect. My actions put me and those around me at risk. When I don't control my emotions, someone has to show me how to make better decisions.

What should I do?

When I am in stressful situations, I will monitor my feelings better and use calming strategies to control my emotions. I can silently count to ten or take deep breaths. If it's okay, I can step away from the situation before I say or do something that will get me into trouble and cause more problems.

What good things will happen to me?

I know that if I can control my emotions, good things will happen to me. When I control my emotions, I stay out of trouble and avoid situations that make it harder for me and others to learn. I won't have to copy this essay again, and I will show others I am mature, responsible, and respectful.

Refraining from Bullying Others

DIRECTIONS: Sit quietly and copy the following essay questions and answers on a separate sheet of paper. Print or write neatly. When finished, raise your hand and be prepared to discuss the essay.

What is Bullying?

Bullying is an act of hurting or intimidating another person. Sometimes we know when we are bullying others and sometimes we do not. Examples include name calling, saying or writing inappropriate things about others, leaving others out of activities, ignoring others, threatening others, making others feel uncomfortable or scared, taking or damaging others' possessions, hitting or kicking others, and making others do things they don't want to do.

What did you do to bully another person?

I bullied another student by...(insert actions here).

Why is it wrong to bully others?

Although bullying can sometimes get me attention or my way during a situation, I am hurting another person in the process. I know I can get along with others. Bullying may make the other person feel lonely, frightened, or sick. The person may feel unsafe around me or others. He or she may think there is something wrong with him or her and may not want to go to school any more. If I continue to bully, I may end up suspended again, my teachers or parents may be disappointed in me, and other students may not trust or like being around me. Sometimes I get things when I bully others but people do not like being true friends with someone who is mean and makes others unhappy. If I continue to bully, I could get into really bad trouble.

REFRAINING FROM BULLYING OTHERS (continued)

What should I do?

If I see someone else being bullied, I should try to stop it and report it to an adult. I am going to act like a hero. I will catch myself when I am bullying, apologize to the person, and find a better way to get what I want without hurting someone else or getting into trouble. I will try to be nice instead.

I know how to be nice, get along with others even if I do not like them, accept "No" answers from others, and act maturely. Even if I want to bully others, I won't do it. I will tell myself to "stop" and I will walk away or find another way to get what I want. Then I won't be in trouble or have to answer essay questions.

What will happen if I am kind instead?

If I am kind, others will like me. I won't be in trouble or be suspended. My teachers will like me and say how proud they are of how I am acting. Other kids won't fight with me or be afraid of me. I will have many true friends and I won't get into trouble again.

Positive Peer Relations

DIRECTIONS: Read the following information and write out your answers.

I got into trouble because of negative peer relations. There is something that needs to change so that I can do better in the future. When I have negative peer relations, I am saying things to people to make them mad and I am treating them with disrespect rather than respect. I am acting immature and irresponsible to my peers and adults.

There are lots of other ways to deal with peer relations in a positive way. If I keep having negative peer relations, other people may be affected. I could lose friends if I yell and scream at them. When I have negative peer relations, I should go talk to a responsible adult or even a good friend who can give me advice about what to do. I should never try to handle a really bad situation by myself. If I want to talk to a peer I am having difficulty with, I can do the following things:

1. I can try to respectfully resolve the conflict, but an adult's help may be needed. I can talk with a teacher, parent, counselor, or other adult if I need help. They can help without me getting into trouble.

2. When I have good peer relations, I will be able to show others I can be a good friend and get along with my peers. I may also have friends who will want to be around me. Adults in my life will likely be proud of who I am and how I act.

List the characteristic of a good friend:_____

_____

In what ways could you become a better friend?_____

_____

In what ways could you avoid conflict with your peers? _____

_____

POSITIVE PEER RELATIONS (continued)

Pick the most important characteristic of being a good friend. Write how you show this characteristic and how you consider this characteristic when choosing friends. _____

_____

_____

_____

Good friends are there to support you through the good and the bad times. Good friends encourage you to make good decisions, keep you out of trouble, and make you feel good about yourself. Negative friends let you down, stir up drama, and encourage poor choices.

DIRECTIONS: List the initials of all your close friends, identify how they affect you in a positive and negative way, and identify whether you should work to strengthen this friendship.			
My Friend	**Negative effects on my life**	**Positive effects on my life**	**How much do I want to strengthen this friendship?** RATE 1-10
Example: T.J.	Wants me to be mean to others, talks behind my back, flirts with the guy I like.	Protects me from other girls, makes me feel good about myself, is there for me when I need her.	4

POSITIVE PEER RELATIONS (continued)

DIRECTIONS: Identify three peers who are not very close friends of yours who could be a positive influence in your life.			
A potential friend is...	**Possible negative effects on my life**	**Possible positive effects on my life**	**How much do I want to strengthen this friendship?** RATE 1-10
Example: A.S.	May not like me; may treat me like she is better than me	Will help me stay out of trouble, will not fight with me, will help me get better grades, my parents will like her	7

Resolving Conflicts

DIRECTIONS: Read the following information and write out your answers. Most students can identify peers who they often have conflicts with and the locations where they often find themselves in conflicts.

What are the locations where you often have conflicts?

1.

2.

3.

Who are the peers you often find yourself having conflicts with?

1.

2.

3.

Conflicts can be resolved by communicating assertively, disagreeing appropriately with respect, compromising with others, giving in when appropriate, or asking an adult to help resolve the conflict. You also may have successfully resolved a conflict in the past. **What three strategies could you use to resolve future conflicts?**

1.

2.

3.

CHAPTER 6

Aggression toward Property

JOHNNY WAS ASSIGNED TO **PAS** FOR PHYSICAL AGGRESSION TOWARD OTHERS AND SCHOOL PROPERTY. In the past month, he has had repeated office referrals for fighting with other students and destruction of school property. During the most recent incident, Johnny was out of his seat during instructional time. Ms. Kent directed Johnny to take a seat. He did so but began kicking a neighbor's desk. Ms. Kent redirected Johnny and instructed him to stop kicking the desk. Johnny stood up, walked out of the room, slammed the door, and kicked and punched several lockers in the hallway, disrupting other classrooms. He also began yelling in the hallway. Ms. Kent escorted Johnny to the office where he calmed down. When he was assigned to PAS as a consequence, he yelled, "She should stay out of my business!" Staff met with Johnny's father and he reported these aggressive behaviors occur frequently at home, too. Johnny understood that his actions resulted in a placement in PAS.

During PAS, Johnny will work on the following skills:

* Accepting Criticism or Consequence
* Disagreeing Appropriately
* Showing Respect
* Accepting Decisions of Authority
* Making an Apology
* Using Anger Control Strategies
* Making Restitution
* Dealing with Frustration

Avoiding Acts of Aggression

> **DIRECTIONS:** Read the following information and write out your answers.

1. **What did you do to get suspended?**

   _____

   _____

   _____

   _____

2. **How did the person(s) respond? How did the person(s) feel?**

   _____

   _____

   _____

   _____

3. **Why did you lose control and damage property?** *(Circle all that apply)*

   - Everyone does it
   - It can be fun
   - It makes me popular
   - Others expect me to be aggressive
   - It makes me feel better
   - People notice me more when I am aggressive
   - I get really angry

AVOIDING ACTS OF AGGRESSION (continued)

> **DIRECTIONS:** Read the sentences on this page, match them with the items you circled on the previous page, and answer the following questions as completely as possible. It will help you think more clearly about what drives your behavior.

4. Everyone does it

Although it may seem like everyone is aggressive at times, only a small number of students damage property and many do it only because they think others want them to do it.

Should you follow the crowd and damage property? Explain your answer. _____

_____

_____

What will happen if you don't follow the crowd?

Good Outcomes: _____

_____

Bad Outcomes: _____

_____

5. It can be fun

Some report that it feels good to have power or control. If you use your strengths, you can discover you are powerful and have control in other ways.

Why is aggression/property damage fun? _____

_____

_____

Do you remember a time when it wasn't fun? _____

_____

_____

6. It makes me popular

When students are aggressive they become less popular with some and more popular with others.

What friends would you lose if you aren't aggressive? _____

_____

_____

What friends would you be less popular with because you are aggressive? _____

_____

_____

7. Others expect me to be aggressive

Sometimes the students who are your friends can pressure you to do things you are not comfortable with or you may get in trouble for doing.

How do your friends pressure you to be aggressive? _____

_____

_____

What would happen if you chose not to be aggressive to others? _____

_____

_____

What could you say or do when you choose not to act aggressively or damage property? _____

_____

_____

8. It makes me feel better

Some students report that being aggressive makes them feel better; however, getting in trouble or losing privileges doesn't feel good. Planning alternative ways of feeling good instead of being aggressive may increase your success in the future.

If you had other ways of feeling good, would you use them? Why would you use them? _____

_____

_____

AVOIDING ACTS OF AGGRESSION (continued)

What are some things you could do to relieve unpleasant feelings or create happiness other than damaging property? (For example: take a walk, exercise, listen to music, count to 10 or 100, talk with a friend, tell a teacher.) _____

_____

_____

Sometimes, students get more attention for being aggressive. We get support from some and attention from the fear felt by others.

How does being aggressive bring you attention from others? _____

_____

_____

What ways could you be noticed without being aggressive or damaging property?_____

_____

_____

9.   What have you learned?

As you reflect on what you have learned about your past behavior, write about why you think you have been aggressive toward property and others._____

_____

_____

_____

_____

Part of growing from an experience is to recognize how to make better choices in the future. Write about what alternatives you have to aggression and property damage and why they are good alternatives. _____

_____

_____

_____

_____

Avoiding Acts of Aggression

DIRECTIONS: Sit quietly and copy the following essay questions and answers on a separate sheet of paper. Print or write neatly. When finished, raise your hand and be prepared to discuss the essay.

What did I do wrong?

I got into trouble for being aggressive. Now I have to copy this essay. Having to copy this essay is a consequence for physical aggression: one I don't like having to do. I need more help in learning to improve my behavior. I have an apology to write, rehearse, and deliver. There will be daily contact with my parent/guardian to report my behaviors. The next time this behavior occurs, even more serious consequences may happen to me.

Why Is It Wrong?

I know it is wrong to be aggressive. It sets a bad example for those younger than me and it is not friendly. I eventually could lose my friends because "nobody likes someone who hurts others." Hurting others could get me into very serious trouble. Other kids will become afraid of me. Other people have to spend time helping me correct my behaviors when they could be using that time for a more useful purpose. It wastes my time, too, because I have to copy this essay.

What Should I Do?

What I should do from now on is be respectful to others and ask adults to help me resolve any conflict I have. I know how to get along with others and not be aggressive. By getting along with others, being friendly, and accepting "No" from people who do not want to do something, I will be acting maturely and responsibly. Even if I feel like being aggressive, I am not going to do it. I'll walk away quietly and will say to myself, "STOP! I am not going to hurt others for any reason. It is not responsible or grown up." That way, I won't be in trouble and I won't have to write this essay.

What Will Happen If I Don't Display Aggression?

I know if I behave responsibly others will like me. My parents will be pleased and think I am being responsible. Other kids won't be afraid of me. I will have many friends and I won't get into trouble.

CHAPTER 7

Impulse Control

RACHEL EARNED A REFERRAL TO **PAS** FOR MAKING INAPPROPRIATE STATEMENTS DURING HER ENGLISH CLASS. Rachel has a history of office referrals for talking out in class and making inappropriate statements to others. During this incident, another student accidentally pushed her desk up against Rachel's desk who turned around and said, "Stop it, b---h." The teacher provided a classroom consequence for Rachel's comment and she was directed to continue working on the current assignment. A bit later, Rachel began talking to her neighbors and was redirected again by the teacher. Rachel impulsively talked out three more times without consideration for the warning and consequences given by the teacher. After the third incident, the teacher privately talked with Rachel, discussed a consequence, and gave her a final warning that the next she talked out during class, she would earn an office referral. During the conversation, Rachel talked over her teacher several times. At that point, the teacher instructed Rachel to stay in her seat, remain quiet, and complete her assignment. After approximately two minutes, Rachel was caught walking to a friend's desk. When the teacher confronted Rachel about this misbehavior, she said, "Oh s--t! I forgot." Given this incident and Rachel's history of office referrals for talking out and not following classroom rules, she was assigned to PAS. Staff met with Rachel's mother who reported Rachel is constantly getting into trouble at home, breaking things, and continues to talk and argue when instructed to stop. A referral was made to the school psychologist and Rachel's parents decided they wanted her to attend PAS as a consequence and to learn new skills to help control her behavior.

During PAS, Rachel will work on the following skills:
* Following Instructions
* Accepting Criticism or a Consequence
* Concentrating on a Subject or Task
* Displaying Effort
* Completing Tasks
* Controlling Emotions
* Choosing Appropriate Words to Say
* Complying with Reasonable Requests
* Showing Respect

Controlling Impulses

DIRECTIONS: Read the following information and write out your answers.

1. **What did you do to get into trouble?**

_____

_____

_____

_____

_____

_____

2. **How did others respond? How do you think they felt?**

_____

_____

_____

_____

_____

_____

3. **Why did you do it?** *(Circle all that apply)*

   - Everyone does it
   - It can be fun
   - It makes me popular
   - Others expect me to be disruptive and not control my impulses
   - It makes me feel better
   - People notice me more when I don't control my impulses

CONTROLLING IMPULSES (continued)

4. Everyone does it

Would you follow the crowd by choosing not to control impulses? Although sometimes it feels like everyone is off task, only a small number of students get into trouble. Usually kids try to get others off task but aren't around when they get into trouble.

What will happen if you don't follow the crowd?

Good Outcomes: _____

_____

_____

_____

Bad Outcomes: _____

_____

_____

_____

_____

5. It can be fun

Sometimes students feel strong when they disrupt class or don't control their impulses. Sometimes they would rather get into trouble than to feel weak. Controlling our impulses and feeling good about ourselves without disrupting others is another way of being strong.

Why is disrupting class fun for you? _____

_____

_____

Do you remember a time when it wasn't fun? _____

_____

_____

_____

Do you think it is fun for others in class? Explain why. _____

_____

_____

CONTROLLING IMPULSES (continued)

6. It makes me popular

When students disrupt class and don't control their impulses they become less popular with some and more popular with others.

What friends would you lose if you chose to control your impulses? _____

_____

_____

_____

7. Others expect me to be disruptive and not control my impulses

Sometimes students who are your friends can pressure you to do something you are uncomfortable with or you may get in trouble for doing.

How do your friends pressure you to not control your impulses?_____

_____

_____

_____

What would happen if you chose to control your impulses? _____

_____

_____

_____

What could you say or do when you decide to control your impulses? _____

_____

_____

_____

_____

What friends like you for who you are and don't pressure you to not control your impulses? _____

_____

_____

_____

CONTROLLING IMPULSES (continued)

8. It makes me feel better

Some students report not controlling their impulses makes them feel better; however, getting in trouble or losing privileges doesn't feel good. Planning alternative ways of feeling good rather than being disruptive may increase your success in the future.

If you had other ways of feeling good would you use them? Why would you use them? _____

_____

_____

_____

_____

_____

What are some things you could do to relieve unpleasant feelings or create happiness other than not controlling impulses? (Examples: take a walk, exercise, listen to music, count to 10 or 100, talk with a friend, tell a teacher.) _____

_____

_____

_____

_____

_____

CONTROLLING IMPULSES (continued)

9. People notice me more when I am disruptive or don't control my impulses

Sometimes students get more attention for disruptions. They get respect from others who don't control their impulses and are liked by others.

How does not controlling impulses bring you attention from others? _____

_____

_____

_____

What ways could you be noticed without disrupting class and controlling impulses? _____

_____

_____

_____

10. What have I learned?

Part of growing from an experience is to recognize how to make better choices in the future.
Write about the alternatives you have to being disruptive and why they are good alternatives.

Write about the alternatives you have to control your impulses and why they are good alternatives.

_____

_____

_____

_____

Controlling Impulses

DIRECTIONS: Read the following information and be prepared to discuss it.

Students who act impulsively report an urge, itch, or sensation right before being impulsive. It can be very difficult to identify this feeling because it mostly occurs unnoticed. "Urge searching" can help a person identify the urge feeling, get used to it, and stop the impulse.

Try to sit completely still for one minute. Notice the feeling of an urge, itch, or sensation to move, say, or do something. Write about what you notice on a separate piece of paper.

Sometimes, we can actively do things to keep ourselves from letting the urge take control. For example, some students purse their lips as a way to stop the urge to talk back or argue with their teacher.

What is something you could actively do in the following situations to help prevent yourself from following an impulse that would get you into trouble? *Write your answers on a separate piece of paper.*

* Arguing when being talked to by an adult

* Talking out or making noises in class

* Inappropriately touching or hitting a peer

* Stealing someone's belongings

* Cheating on a test or homework by looking over at another person's desk

* Getting up in class when the rules are to remain seated

* Tapping or making noise with your hands or feet

Example of "How to Fight the Urge": put your hands in your pockets, purse your lips, flex your throat muscles, hold on to your desk, keep both hands on an object like a pencil, stare at your desk or a teacher, stay away from others' belongings, clasp your hands together, flex your neck muscles slightly to keep your head toward the front of the classroom.

_____   _____

SIGNATURE   DATE

CHAPTER 8

Stealing/Dishonesty

NATASHA WAS SUSPENDED FROM SCHOOL FOR TAKING A TEACHER'S CELL PHONE FROM HER DESK. Natasha showed the phone to some other girls in the restroom and one of the girls reported the theft to Mr. Mathews, who went to Natasha's science class and asked her to hand over the phone she had in her possession. Natasha surrendered the phone but said she didn't know how it got into her bag. Mr. Mathews discussed with Natasha that being in possession of stolen property is a serious violation of the code of conduct. She was assigned to PAS.

During PAS, Natasha will work on the following skills:

* Following Rules
* Controlling the Impulse to Steal
* Making Decisions
* Making an Apology
* Dealing with an Accusation
* Making Restitution
* Borrowing from Others

Communicating Honestly / Controlling Impulse to Steal

DIRECTIONS: Below are a series of statements and questions. Read them carefully and write (or check) your answers in the space provided. Use complete sentences and be prepared to discuss your answers.

| **Honesty is expected at school. Today, I was not honest and/or I stole. Stealing at school will get me into trouble. In the past, I…** | Have stolen from someone at school |
| | Have not stolen from someone at school |

There are many reasons why it is important to be honest at school. Honesty is an important character trait. Some of the reasons why I should be honest and not steal at school are:

- When I steal, people are less likely to trust me in the future.
- Stealing damages my reputation, and it takes time to earn trust again.
- I show courage and trustworthiness when I tell the truth.
- Being honest can solve problems more quickly, which helps save time.
- Being honest can help me avoid bigger consequences later.

Being honest is particularly important to me for two reasons
(choose two from the previous list or write your own reasons):

COMMUNICATING HONESTLY / CONTROLLING IMPULSE TO STEAL (continued)

In the future, I will use the skills of *Communicating Honestly* and *Controlling the Impulse to Steal*. The steps to the skills are:

Communicating Honestly	Controlling the Impulse to Steal
1. Look at the person.	1. Identify and avoid situations in which you are likely to steal.
2. Use a clear voice. Avoid stammering or hesitating.	2. Before you steal, stop your behavior immediately.
3. Respond to questions factually and completely.	3. Instruct yourself to leave the area without stealing.
4. Do not leave out details or important facts.	4. Consider the long-term consequences of stealing.
5. Truthfully take responsibility for any inappropriate behaviors you displayed.	5. Self-report any previous stealing.

In the future, I will try to be more honest at school with identifying situations when I am likely to steal, and I will avoid those situations. I will make sure I am honest and avoid the impulse to steal by... *(describe your specific plan)*

COMMUNICATING HONESTLY / CONTROLLING IMPULSE TO STEAL (continued)

If I need help with telling the truth and avoiding the impulse to steal, I will ask a teacher, counselor, or administrator to help me work on being honest. Or, I will talk to a friend who is trustworthy or ask my family for help. **The people or resources I can use to help me be honest are:**

Between **Communicating Honestly** and **Controlling the Impulse to Steal**, the skill I need the most help with is:

The steps of the skill are:

At school, there are consequences for being dishonest and stealing. Consequences can include correction from a teacher, detention, office referral, in-school suspension, meeting with a teacher or administrator, phone call(s) home, and failing an assignment or class. In addition, there are natural consequences for stealing, including losing friendships, earning a bad reputation, losing the respect of others, and losing the trust of classmates and teachers. **The consequences I want to avoid are:**

COMMUNICATING HONESTLY / CONTROLLING IMPULSE TO STEAL (continued)

DIRECTIONS: You may need to refer to the previous pages to answer the following questions. For each question, write a response using at least two complete sentences. If your answers are not written appropriately (capitalization, punctuation, and readable handwriting), you may have to redo the worksheet.

What are two reasons why it is better to be honest with others than to lie?

How does lying affect your school behavior?

What two actions or steps can you take to communicate honestly in the future?

There may be more consequences in the future for lies or dishonesty.
What are two possible consequences?

What are two benefits or good things that can happen when communicating honestly and telling the truth?

COMMUNICATING HONESTLY / CONTROLLING IMPULSE TO STEAL (continued)

DIRECTIONS: Read the following quotes about honesty and then complete the sentences by writing your answers in the space provided. Use complete sentences and proper punctuation.

The quote I like best is…		
		"Truth might be unattainable, but honesty is not." – STEPHEN WATSON, SOUTH AFRICAN POET
		"Honesty is the best policy. If I lose mine honor, I lose myself." – WILLIAM SHAKESPEARE, ENGLISH POET AND PLAYWRIGHT
		"Honesty is the first chapter in the book of wisdom." – THOMAS JEFFERSON, UNITED STATES PRESIDENT
		"Oh what a tangled web we weave, when first we practice to deceive." – SIR WALTER SCOTT, SCOTTISH WRITER AND POET

I think this quote means:

The reason I like the quote is:

In my job as a student, I can demonstrate honesty by:

_____   _____

SIGNATURE   DATE

Communicating Honestly / Controlling Impulse to Steal

DIRECTIONS: Read the following sentences carefully and answer by filling in the blanks or writing in the space provided. Please use complete sentences.

What behavior led to this consequence?

What were you thinking or feeling at the time?

What did you want to happen?

Did you get what you wanted?

What did it cost you?

What alternative(s) could you choose next time to avoid a consequence?

MEDIATION ESSAY

Controlling Impulse to Steal

DIRECTIONS: Sit quietly and answer the following essay questions on a separate sheet of paper. Print or write neatly. When finished, raise your hand and be prepared to discuss the essay.

What did I do wrong?

Why is stealing wrong?

What should I do instead?

What will happen to me if I can stop myself from stealing?

Controlling Impulse to Steal

What did I do wrong?

I took something that did not belong to me. I took something that was the property of someone else.

I need more help in learning to improve my behavior. Besides copying this paper, I have to agree in a written contract to show improvement in my stealing behavior for 10 days in a row. The contract will go home for my parents to read and sign. And, I have to deliver an apology to the person I stole from.

If I behave this way again, other consequences may happen to me. I may have to spend time in detention. My parents may be asked to come to school for a conference.

Why is stealing wrong?

If I take things that belong to other people, they are going to be mad at me and not like me. They'll call me a "thief" or a "stealer." When other kids find out I take things that aren't mine, I could lose friends. I could also get hurt if the person gets mad at me and hits me. If I take things that aren't mine, I'll get into trouble with the teacher and principal. My parents will be disappointed in me, too, when they find out. If I get in the habit of stealing, I'll get into big trouble with the police.

What should I do instead?

I shouldn't take things that don't belong to me. If I see something I'd like to have and feel like I'm going to take it, I have to tell myself, "STOP! I can't take that! It doesn't belong to me!" After I tell myself to stop and not take the thing I want to steal, I have to get myself away from that place/item and go someplace where there are people around.

CONTROLLING IMPULSE TO STEAL (continued)

What will happen to me if I can stop myself from stealing?

If I don't steal, I won't get into trouble with my parents or teachers. Other kids won't be afraid that I'll take something of theirs, and they will like and trust me. If I can stop myself from stealing now, I won't have trouble with stealing when I get older. If I can stop stealing, I can show people that I am responsible and that I can take care of myself.

CHAPTER 9

Substances/ Weapons/Contraband

ZEKE DETONATED A STINK BOMB IN AN AUDIO-VISUAL CLOSET IN THE CAFETERIA DURING LUNCH. This caused the cafeteria to fill up with a foul odor, disrupted the lunch routine for staff and students, and posed a health risk to others. When questioned by four administrators on four different occasions, Zeke denied any involvement. He said he did not know anything about it and attempted to implicate another student. Eventually, his involvement was uncovered when Zeke bragged about detonating the stink bomb on a social media site and that another student was taking the "fall." Zeke wrote, "Russel is king! Thanks for taking the heat off me for the stink bomb!" Only after being confronted with the writing did Zeke eventually admit he was the one who did it. He reported to PAS to work on avoiding bringing contraband to school and honesty.

During PAS, Zeke will work on the following skills:

* Controlling the Impulse to Lie
* Refraining from Possessing Contraband and Drugs
* Following Safety Rules
* Preventing Trouble with Others
* Resisting Peer Pressure
* Seeking Positive Attention
* Choosing Appropriate Friends
* Communicating Honestly
* Dealing with Group Pressure
* Keeping Property in its Place
* Making Decisions
* Making Restitution
* Self-Reporting Own Behaviors
* Being an Appropriate Role Model

Refraining from Possessing Substances / Weapons / Contraband

> **DIRECTIONS:** Read the following information and write out your answers.

1. **What did you do to get into trouble?**

   _____

   _____

   _____

2. **How did you and other people get hurt by this situation (loss of respect, loss of friends, loss of trust, etc.)?**

   - You? _____

   _____

   _____

   - The other people involved?_____

   _____

   _____

3. **Why did you do it?** *(Circle all that apply)*

   - Everyone does it
   - It can be fun
   - It makes me popular
   - Others expect me to do it
   - It makes me feel better
   - People notice me more

   Are there any other reasons that were not listed?

   _____

   _____

REFRAINING FROM POSSESSING SUBSTANCES / WEAPONS / CONTRABAND (continued)

DIRECTIONS: Read the following information and answer the questions as completely as possible. It will help you think more clearly about what drives your behavior.

4. Everyone does it

Would you follow the crowd by breaking the same rules again? _____

_____

_____

_____

What will happen if you don't follow the crowd?

Good Outcomes: _____

_____

Bad Outcomes: _____

_____

5. It can be fun

Why is it fun? _____

_____

_____

_____

Do you remember a time when it wasn't fun? _____

Do you think it is fun for everyone? Tell why. _____

_____

_____

_____

REFRAINING FROM POSSESSING SUBSTANCES/WEAPONS/CONTRABAND (continued)

How has it hurt you? _____

_____

_____

_____

How has it hurt others? _____

_____

_____

_____

6. It makes me popular

When students break serious school rules, they become less popular with some groups and more popular with others.

What friends would you lose if you choose not to break rules again? _____

_____

_____

_____

What friends have you become less popular with because of what you have done? _____

_____

_____

_____

7. Others expect me to do it

How do your friends pressure you to do the behaviors that get you in trouble? _____

_____

_____

_____

REFRAINING FROM POSSESSING SUBSTANCES / WEAPONS / CONTRABAND (continued)

What would happen if you chose not to do it again? _____

_____

_____

_____

What could you say when you tell others that you are not doing it again? _____

_____

_____

_____

8. It makes me feel better

Some students report that breaking rules makes them feel better; however, getting in trouble or losing privileges doesn't feel good. Planning alternative ways of feeling good rather than breaking major school rules may increase your success in the future.

If you had positive, alternative ways of feeling good, would you use them? Why would you use them?

_____

_____

_____

What are some things you could do to relieve unpleasant feelings other than breaking the school rules? (For example: take a walk, exercise, listen to music, count to 10 or 100, talk with a friend, tell a teacher)

_____

_____

_____

9. People notice me more when I do break rules

How does breaking a school rule bring you attention from others? _____

_____

_____

_____

REFRAINING FROM POSSESSING SUBSTANCES/WEAPONS/CONTRABAND (continued)

What ways could you get noticed without breaking school rules? _____

_____

_____

_____

10. What have I learned?

Part of growing from an experience is to recognize how to make better choices in the future.

If you had the chance to redo the incident that you were referred for, how would you act differently?

_____

_____

_____

Who can you talk with for help or support if you notice yourself wanting to do this again? _____

_____

_____

_____

Refraining from Possessing Contraband

DIRECTIONS: Read the following sentences carefully and answer by filling in the blanks or writing in the space provided. Please use complete sentences.

I violated a school policy when I… (describe the situation): _____

_____

_____

_____

The reason why I had contraband was: _____

_____

_____

_____

List three ways you can avoid this problem in the future, then circle the best one:

1. _____

_____

_____

2. _____

_____

_____

3. _____

_____

_____

Refraining from Possessing Contraband

DIRECTIONS: Read the following paragraphs and be prepared to have a discussion with your teacher or administrator.

Possessing contraband violates my school's policy about what items are acceptable on school grounds. Having illegal, stolen, or morally inappropriate items at school creates a dangerous and unhealthy environment for all students and staff. When I ignore this policy, I put my future at risk. I can be suspended or expelled. A suspension will make it harder for me to keep up with schoolwork. An expulsion means I will have to finish the school year somewhere else, and I will miss out on spending time with friends and having access to academic resources. Also, the police might get involved, and I may end up in juvenile detention or on probation. **However, if I follow the rules and policies of the school, I can avoid negative consequences and help keep my school safe for students and staff.**

When I'm older, the consequences can be more serious if I possess drugs or have illegal contraband. I can get arrested and have a permanent police record, which can make it harder for me to obtain a driver's license, get a job, or rent an apartment. My reputation and personal relationships also can suffer. **However, if I am responsible and keep away from illegal activities and items, such as drug possession and possession of stolen property, I can avoid a criminal record and unnecessary hardships.**

I understand my teacher is trying to help me stay safe and away from illegal or inappropriate activities and items that might jeopardize my future. I also know my decision will have consequences. If I violate this school policy again, I will earn more negative consequences.

I will strive to do better in the future.

_____   _____
SIGNATURE   DATE

Refraining from Possessing Substances / Weapons / Contraband

DIRECTIONS: Sit quietly and answer the following essay questions on a separate sheet of paper. Print or write neatly. When finished, raise your hand and be prepared to discuss the essay.

What did I do wrong?
What could happen to me?
Why was it wrong?
What should I do?
What good things will happen to me?

Refraining from Possessing Substances / Weapons / Contraband

What did I do wrong?

I got into trouble for bringing something to school that was not allowed. Now I have to copy this essay. Having to copy this essay is a consequence for bringing something that was not allowed to school. I need more help in learning to improve my behavior. I have to write an apology, rehearse it, and deliver it. There will be daily contact with my parent/guardian to report my behaviors. The next time this behavior occurs, even more serious consequences may happen to me. Specifically, I (insert what was brought to school) which is against the rules and wrong of me to bring.

Why is it wrong?

I know it is wrong to violate the school rules and bring something that is not allowed at school. It sets a bad example for those younger than me, and it is not considerate to my teachers or friends. I could eventually lose the respect of my teachers and friends because I broke a serious rule. Bringing things that are not allowed at school makes friends and teachers uncomfortable and sometimes scared. Now other people have to spend time helping me correct my behaviors when they could spend this time doing something more fun. It wastes my time because I have to copy this essay and be in a program away from my friends.

What should I do?

What I should do from now on is not violate the school rules and never bring items that are not allowed at school again. If I am having difficulties at school, I should talk with an adult at home or school to help me resolve my problems. If my so called "friends" are urging me do it, I will tell them "No" and will also tell an adult because I am not their puppet. I won't be in trouble because of someone else's funny idea. Even if I want to bring something that is not allowed at school, I won't do it. I will tell myself "STOP!" And I will walk away and find another way to get what I want. That way, I won't get in trouble or have to rewrite this essay.

REFRAINING FROM POSSESSING SUBSTANCES / WEAPONS / CONTRABAND (continued)

What will happen if I don't bring these items to school in the future?

If I don't bring inappropriate items to school then my teachers and real friends will like me. I can gain others' respect and friendship without breaking the school rules. I can ask a teacher to help me get involved in ways that gain respect. Teachers were kids once, too, and I know some care about me and would help. If I see someone else bring items that are not allowed at school, I should tell an adult. I am going to be a helper and a hero.

SECTION 4
Reentry

✳ ✳ ✳

Making an Apology

✱ Lesson Plan

Administrator/Staff/Interventionist Notes

ACTS OF KINDNESS HELP STUDENTS BUILD HEALTHIER, MORE RESPECTFUL RELATIONSHIPS WITH ADULTS AND EACH OTHER. One act of kindness is admitting mistakes and saying, "I'm sorry." Behavioral mistakes, disagreements, accidents, and misunderstandings do happen at school. If students never apologize or seem insincere when they do, an environment of resentment and bitterness can easily develop between students and staff. In such an unforgiving atmosphere, behavior problems and classroom disruptions can occur with greater frequency.

Using the Boys Town Education Model's PAS process means students are expected to use the skill of "Making an Apology" to earn their way back into the classroom. By teaching students how to make an apology, you reinforce the behavior expectations and policies of the school.

Have students practice an apology they can deliver to their teachers or the persons they hurt or offended before returning them to class. The following lesson plan, role-play scenarios, and Think Sheet can be used to guide students in developing their apologies.

✳ Planned Teaching Interaction

Introduce the Skill

Start by telling students that it is time to practice the skill of Making an Apology, and remind them that an apology is part of their consequence. Tell them they need to practice this skill now because they will need to make an apology to their teachers before being allowed back in the classroom. You also might mention other reasons for why it's important to practice how to make an apology. Reasons can include:

* Shows maturity

* Helps repair relationships

* Provides resolution

* Shows respect

Describe the Appropriate Behavior or Skill Steps

Making an Apology (Saying You're Sorry)

1. **Look at the person.**

    * Eye contact shows respect for the person receiving the apology and helps communicate your sincerity.

    * Have a pleasant or neutral facial expression; avoid frowning or laughing.

2. **Use a serious, sincere voice tone but don't pout.**

    * An appropriate voice tone communicates to the person your apology is genuine.

    * Avoid using a tone that sounds condescending, dismissive, or phony.

132

3. **Begin by saying, "I want to apologize for…."**
   Or "I'm sorry for…."

   * Say specifically what you did that caused the pain, hurt, or embarrassment.

4. **Do not make excuses or try to rationalize your behavior.**

   * Own up to your actions.

5. **Sincerely say you will try not to repeat the same behavior in the future.**

   * Say what you will do in the future to avoid repeating the same mistake.

6. **Offer to compensate or pay restitution.**

   * Sometimes saying you're sorry won't be enough, especially if property, such as books or clothes, are damaged or destroyed.

7. **Thank the other person for listening.**

Give a Reason or Rationale

Everyone at times makes errors in judgment or does something that hurts or disappoints others. When you can recognize such mistakes or realize when you have "goofed," you can try to correct the situation and soothe hurt feelings. Making an apology is the first step. It may not always make everything okay, but it starts the healing process. Other benefits of knowing how to make an apology include:

* Apologizing is a necessary skill for maintaining friendships.

* An apology shows that you recognize your mistakes and are mature enough to admit them.

* Apologies can help others forgive you and your mistake, and make it less likely they will carry a grudge or remain upset.

* By not offering an apology, you can damage relationships and make future interactions more difficult.

✳ Practice

Have students select one of the following scenarios to role-play with you.

1. You argued with your teacher about how she graded your essay. You constantly interrupted her and disrupted the classroom. Following the steps of the skill, show how you would apologize for your behavior.

2. In the cafeteria, a group of students were taunting and laughing at one of your friends. You pretended not to notice what was happening and walked away. Your friend saw you leave and is hurt and angry because you didn't help. Describe how you would apologize and say you're sorry.

3. Your classroom teacher is out ill and you have a substitute teacher for the day. When the substitute has her back turned, you make faces and imitate her actions. When she turns around suddenly, she catches you making fun of her. Respond by apologizing and saying you're sorry.

4. You didn't do your chores around the house and were grounded for the weekend. You were so angry you yelled at your mom and said things you wish you could take back. To repair your relationship with her, show and say you're sorry.

5. You were warned not to talk during a class lecture. You did anyway, got caught, and earned an office referral. Show how you would return to the classroom and apologize to the teacher for disrupting the class and not following the rules.

✳ Provide Additional Support

Use the following worksheets to help reinforce the importance of the skill *Making an Apology.*

Making an Apology

DIRECTIONS: Read the following questions and write out your answers.

NAME: DATE:

List times or situations where making an apology and saying you're sorry are important in school and outside of school:

1. _____

_____

_____

2. _____

_____

_____

3. _____

_____

_____

Why should you learn how to make an apology? _____

_____

_____

Describe the situation that led to your suspension: _____

_____

_____

_____

MAKING AN APOLOGY (continued)

What did you do to make the situation worse? _____

_____

_____

What could you have done to handle the situation better? _____

_____

_____

When making an apology, you should include the following:
- Make a statement of regret. ("I am sorry for....")
- Make a plan for next time. ("Next time, I will....")
- Ask questions, including:
  - "Do you accept my apology?"
  - "Can I come back to class?"
  - "Did I miss any work?"
- Say "thanks" because the person you apologized to listened to you and/or accepted your apology.

Write out an apology for the situation you got in trouble for: _____

_____

_____

How can the skill of **Making an Apology (Saying You're Sorry)** help you in this situation? _____

_____

_____

How can the skill of **Making an Apology (Saying You're Sorry)** help you in other situations? _____

_____

_____

_____

✳ Conclusion

When working with students who earn suspensions, keep in mind their behavior is learned and learning replacement behaviors may be a long process for some. The learning process may start out with small approximations of the replacement behavior, which can then be shaped over time. The PAS program is a way for you to correct inappropriate behaviors that frequently lead to suspensions and intentionally use resources to teach alternative positive behaviors and skills. In addition, the PAS program helps you to reduce the number of suspensions issued because you are teaching students replacement behaviors and helping them keep up academically. This is especially important because falling behind academically is an often overlooked reason for repeated suspensions.

SECTION 5
Additional Resources

✳ ✳ ✳

This section contains additional resources PAS supervisors can use during the PAS process. If a student's misbehavior doesn't fit into one of the previous chapters, a great way to problem solve and create additional discussions is to use the SODAS or POP problem-solving worksheets. This can help students identify and practice better choices in future situations. Also included are behavioral worksheets that focus on typical antecedent behaviors that many students who earn frequent suspensions deal with, including assignment competition, time management, and others. You can look through this section to find skills and resources that may be appropriate for your students to learn and practice. The forms can be used as standalone resources or in conjunction with the resources provided in the previous chapters.

Forms

ALONG WITH THE FORMS PRESENTED IN THE PREVIOUS CHAPTERS, ADMINISTRATORS MAY FIND FORMS IN THIS SECTION HELPFUL IN DEALING WITH COMMON BEHAVIORAL CHALLENGES. At the end of the section, you will find blank forms that can be printed and customized to meet the needs of your students. All forms are also available to print and download using the instructions provided below:

Access:

http://www.boystowntraining.org/btpdownloads.html
(Please note: The web address must include .html at the end.)

Enter:

Your first and last names
Email address
Product code: 934490pas990

Solving Problems with SODAS

DIRECTIONS: Read the following sentences carefully and answer by filling in the blanks or writing in the space provided. Please use complete sentences.

Situation	Describe your problem or situation here.
Options	Make a list of ways you could solve the problem. OPTION #1:
	OPTION #2:
	OPTION #3:

SOLVING PROBLEMS WITH SODAS (continued)

Disadvantages and Advantages	List advantages and disadvantages of each option.
	OPTION #1: Disadvantages: Advantages:
	OPTION #2: Disadvantages: Advantages::
	OPTION #3: Disadvantages: Advantages:
Solution	Decide which option represents the best possible solution. Briefly describe how you will put your plan to work to solve the problem.

Solving Problems with POP
Problem * Options * Plan

DIRECTIONS: Read the following sentences carefully and answer by filling in the blanks or writing in the space provided. Please use complete sentences.

Problem	Describe your problem.
Options	Make a list of ways you could solve the problem and include a possible outcome or result. OPTION #1:
	OPTION #2:
	OPTION #3:
Plan	Decide which option will work best to solve the problem. Briefly describe how you will put your plan to work to solve the problem.

Completing School Work / Assigned Tasks

DIRECTIONS: Below are a series of statements and questions. Read them carefully and write (or check) your answers in the space provided. Use complete sentences and be prepared to discuss your answers.

Schoolwork is part of my job description as a student, and I am expected to do all of the assignments and participate in class. Today, I refused to follow instructions by not doing my assigned work. In the past, I have...		Refused to do my assigned work
		Completed my assigned work

There are many reasons why doing assigned work is important. Some of the reasons why I should participate in class and do assignments are:

- If I do the work when it is assigned, I am more likely to remember how and what to do.
- When I do all of the assignments, I learn the material better and won't fall behind.
- I show respect to my teachers and classmates by doing my job.
- I avoid negative consequences for having incomplete and unfinished work.
- I show others I'm responsible and understand that school is for learning.

Completing school work is particularly important to me for two reasons...
(choose two from the previous list or write your own):

COMPLETING SCHOOL WORK / ASSIGNED TASKS (continued)

In the future, I will do all of my assigned work. I will do this by starting my work promptly, asking for help appropriately, and staying on task. The skills I can use to help me are *Doing Good Quality Work, Using Study Skills,* and *Following Written Instructions.* The steps of the skills are:

Doing Good Quality Work

1. Find out the exact expectations or instructions for tasks; ask for clarification if needed.
2. Assemble the necessary tools or materials.
3. Carefully begin working. Focus your attention on the task.
4. Continue working until the task is completed or criteria are met.
5. Examine the results of your work to make sure it was done correctly.
6. Correct any deficiencies, mistakes, or parts left out.
7. Perhaps, check back with the person who assigned the task.

Using Study Skills

1. Gather the necessary books and materials.
2. Focus your attention on the required academic work.
3. Make notes of important facts.
4. Repeat important points to yourself several times.
5. Remain on task, free from distractions (no radio or TV on).

Following Written Instructions

1. Read the written instructions for the task one time completely.
2. Do what each instruction tells you to in the exact order in which it is written.
3. Don't change written instructions or skip any without permission.
4. If you have any questions, raise your hand or find the appropriate adult to ask about the instructions in question.

COMPLETING SCHOOL WORK / ASSIGNED TASKS (continued)

In the future, I will try to complete all assignments by following instructions, staying on task, and asking for help when I need it. I will make sure I complete my assigned work by… *(describe your specific plan):*

If I need help doing what I need to do when I need to do it, I will ask a teacher or administrator to help me. Or, I will talk to a friend or family member. This shows responsibility, which is an important character trait. **The people or resources I can use to help me stay on task and finish schoolwork are:**

Of the skills **Doing Good Quality Work, Using Study Skills,** and **Following Written Instructions,** the one I need the most help with is:

The steps of the skill are:

At school, there are consequences for refusing to do assigned work. Consequences can include correction from a teacher, detention, office referral, earning an incomplete, meeting with a teacher or administrator, and phone calls home. In addition, there are natural consequences for refusing to do assigned work, including confusion, embarrassment, and loss of respect from peers and teachers. **The consequences I want to avoid are:**

COMPLETING SCHOOL WORK / ASSIGNED TASKS (continued)

> **DIRECTIONS:** You may need to refer to the previous pages to answer the following questions. For each question, write a response using at least two complete sentences. If your answers are not written appropriately (capitalization, punctuation, and readable handwriting), you may have to redo the worksheet.

What are two reasons why it is important to do assigned work in a timely manner?

When you refuse to do school work, how does that hurt you?

What two skills can help you become more responsible and do work when it is assigned?

There may be more consequences in the future if you refuse to do school work. What are two possible consequences?

What are two benefits or good things that can happen when you do your work promptly?

COMPLETING SCHOOL WORK / ASSIGNED TASKS (continued)

> **DIRECTIONS:** Read the following quotes about effort and then complete the sentences by writing your answers in the space provided. Use complete sentences and proper punctuation.

The quote I like best is…		
		"Everything you do sends a message about who you are and what you value." – Michael Josephson, Founder of CHARACTER COUNTS!
		"The only place where success comes before work is in the dictionary." – Vidal Sassoon, Celebrity Hairstylist
		"Hard work spotlights the character of people: some turn up their sleeves, some turn up their noses, and some don't turn up at all." – Sam Ewing, American Author
		"Things may come to those who wait, but only the things left by those who hustle." – Abraham Lincoln, United States President

I think it means:

The reason I like this quote is:

I can apply this quote to my life by doing the following:

_____   _____

SIGNATURE   DATE

Using Appropriate Language

DIRECTIONS: Below are a series of statements and questions. Read them carefully and write (or check) your answers in the space provided. Use complete sentences and be prepared to discuss your answers.

Today, I used inappropriate language at school. Inappropriate language can be cursing, swearing, using derogatory terms, putting others down, or calling others inappropriate names. In the past, I...		Have used inappropriate language
		Have not used inappropriate language

Appropriate language is expected at my school. The student handbook mentions it in several places. There are many reasons why using appropriate language is an important rule at my school. Some of the reasons why I should use **appropriate language** include:

- It is a good habit to develop because using appropriate language is expected in other settings, such as the workplace. School is my workplace.

- I can expand my vocabulary by learning and using appropriate words.

- I can avoid unnecessary misunderstandings when I don't use inappropriate slang or words.

- I show respect to my classmates and teachers when I don't curse or put others down.

- I can avoid negative consequences, including being corrected by a teacher.

- Cursing, profanity, and putdowns create a hostile environment, and my school is supposed to be a safe place for students.

Using appropriate language at school is particularly important to me for two reasons (choose two from the previous list or write your own):

USING APPROPRIATE LANGUAGE (continued)

In the future, I will try to use appropriate language by using the skill of **Choosing Appropriate Words to Say**. The steps of the skill are:

- Look at the situation and the people around you.
- Know the meanings of words you are about to say.
- Refrain from using words that will offend people around you or that they will not understand.
- Avoid using slang, profanity, or words that could have a sexual meaning or are putdowns.
- If you are angry, take deep breaths or walk away from the situation to avoid saying something inappropriate.

Of the five skill steps previously listed, the three I need to improve on the most are:

If I need help choosing appropriate words, I will ask a teacher, administrator, or counselor to help me. Or, I will ask a friend or talk to a family member. **The people or resources I can use to help me are:**

At school, there are consequences for using inappropriate language. Consequences can include correction from a teacher, detention, office referral, in-school suspension, meeting with a teacher or administrator, and phone calls home. In addition, there are natural consequences, including losing the respect of others, earning a bad reputation, being embarrassed, straining relationships, and losing leadership opportunities in class and extracurricular activities. **The consequences I want to avoid are:**

USING APPROPRIATE LANGUAGE (continued)

DIRECTIONS: You may need to refer to the previous pages to answer the following questions. For each question, write a response using at least two complete sentences. If your answers are not written appropriately (capitalization, punctuation, and readable handwriting), you may have to redo the worksheet.

What are two reasons why you should use appropriate language at school and school-sponsored activities?

How are you hurt when you curse, call names, or say derogatory remarks at school?

What two actions or steps do you plan to take to help you use appropriate language at school?

There may be more negative consequences in the future if you curse and use profanity at school. What are two possible consequences?

What are two benefits or good things that can happen when you use appropriate language at school?

_____   _____

SIGNATURE   DATE

Completing Homework on Time

| **Homework is part of my job description as a student, and I am expected to follow all of the instructions when I have homework assignments. Today, I...** | Did not have my homework |
| | Did have my homework |

There are many reasons why my school assigns take-home work. Some of the reasons why it's important for me to do homework are:

- If I do the homework when it is assigned, I will probably do better in class, especially during tests and reviews.
- If I do my homework, I will be less likely to fall behind, my grades won't go down, and I will avoid an incomplete.
- I can show the teacher how well I understand the subject and if I need more instruction or help.
- It shows others I'm responsible and know how to meet deadlines.
- I will develop better study habits and my grades might improve.
- I avoid trouble with my teachers or parents for having late or incomplete work.

Finishing homework on time is particularly important to me for two reasons
(choose two from the previous list or write your own):

COMPLETING HOMEWORK ON TIME (continued)

In the future, I will use the skill of **Completing Homework.** The steps of the skill are:

- Find out at school what the day's homework is for each subject, and write it in my planner.
- Remember to bring home necessary books or materials in order to finish assignments.
- Get started on homework promptly or at the designated time.
- Complete all assignments accurately and neatly.
- Carefully store completed homework until the next school day.
- If I cannot follow these steps because of situations outside of my control, I will ask for help.

Of the six skill steps listed above, the one I struggle with the most is:

In the future, I will do my homework on time. If I don't understand my homework, I will ask questions before I go home. At home, I will ask an older sibling or adult for help. I will set aside a specific time to do homework, and I will make sure I put my homework in my folder or backpack at night. If I am unable to do this because of circumstances outside my control, I will ask a teacher, counselor, or trusted adult for help. I will make sure I finish my homework and turn it in on time by... *(describe your specific plan):*

COMPLETING HOMEWORK ON TIME (continued)

If I need help with the skill, I will ask a teacher, counselor, administrator, or family member for assistance. This shows responsibility, which is an important character trait. **The people or resources I can use to help me complete my homework on time are:**

There are school consequences for not completing homework. The consequences can include correction from a teacher, office referral, detention, low grade or incomplete, meeting with a teacher or administrator, and phone calls home. In addition, there are natural consequences for incomplete or late homework, including falling behind, embarrassment, lost opportunities, confusion, and the loss of respect and trust from adults and peers.
The consequences I want to avoid are:

COMPLETING HOMEWORK ON TIME (continued)

DIRECTIONS: You may need to refer to the previous pages to answer the following questions. For each question, write a response using at least two complete sentences. If your answers are not written appropriately (capitalization, punctuation, and readable handwriting), you may have to redo the worksheet.

What are two reasons why it is important to do homework on time and completely?

How does having late or incomplete homework affect school performance?

What are two actions or steps you can take to be more responsible about homework in the future?

There may be more consequences in the future when homework is late or incomplete. What are two possible consequences?

What are two benefits or good things that can happen when homework is complete and turned in on time?

COMPLETING HOMEWORK ON TIME (continued)

DIRECTIONS: Read the following quotes about effort and then complete the sentences by writing your answers in the space provided. Use complete sentences and proper punctuation.

The quote I like best is…		*"Everything you do sends a message about who you are and what you value."* – MICHAEL JOSEPHSON, FOUNDER OF CHARACTER COUNTS!
		"The only place where success comes before work is in the dictionary." – VIDAL SASSOON, CELEBRITY HAIRSTYLIST
		"Hard work spotlights the character of people: some turn up their sleeves, some turn up their noses, and some don't turn up at all." – SAM EWING, AMERICAN AUTHOR
		"Things may come to those who wait, but only the things left by those who hustle." – ABRAHAM LINCOLN, UNITED STATES PRESIDENT

I think the quote I picked means:

The reason I like this quote is:

In my job as a student, I can demonstrate responsibility with homework by:

SIGNATURE

DATE

Positive Alternatives to Suspension

Being on Time

| **Being on time is a school rule. Today, I was late for class. In the past, I…** | Have been late for my classes |
| | Have been on time for my classes |

There are many reasons why my school has a rule about being on time. Some of the reasons why I should be prompt include:

- The start of class is usually when goals are set and directions are given. I am more likely to do well in class when I don't miss hearing important information.
- Being on time can develop into a habit that will help me in the future.
- I show respect to my classmates by not interrupting class time.
- It shows others I'm responsible and have the time-management skills to be on time.
- I create a safety issue when I do not show up on time.

Two reasons why being on time is particularly important to me are (choose two from the previous list or write your own):

BEING ON TIME (continued)

In the future, I will use the skill of **Being on Time (Promptness)**. The steps of the skill are:

- Know exactly when you need to be where you are going, and how long it will take to get there.
- Leave with plenty of time to spare.
- Go directly to your destination with no diversions.
- If you are late, apologize and follow the school's procedure for tardiness.

In the future, I will try to be on time to school and my classes by planning better, watching the clock during break, or waking up earlier. I will make sure I am on time in the future by… *(describe your specific plan):*

If I need help with this skill, I will ask a teacher or administrator to help me work on being on time. Or, I will talk to a friend who is prompt or ask my family for help. **The people or resources I can use to help me be on time are:**

There are consequences for being late. The consequences can include tardy slips, detention, missing work, falling behind, meeting with a teacher or administrator, and phone calls home. In addition, there are natural consequences for being late, including confusion, embarrassment, misinformation or lack of information, lost opportunities, and the loss of respect and trust from adults and peers. **The consequences I want to avoid are:**

BEING ON TIME (continued)

> **DIRECTIONS:** You may need to refer to the previous pages to answer the following questions. For each question, write a response using at least two complete sentences. If your answers are not written appropriately (capitalization, punctuation, and readable handwriting), you may have to redo the worksheet.

What are two reasons why your school has a rule about being on time?

How is coming late to school or class harmful to you?

What two actions or steps do you intend to take to be prompt and on time?

There may be more negative consequences in the future if you are tardy. What are two other consequences?

What are two benefits or good things that can happen when you come to school or class on time?

_____   _____

SIGNATURE   DATE

Being Prepared for Class

DIRECTIONS: Read the following sentences carefully and answer by filling in the blanks or writing in the space provided. Please use complete sentences.

I failed to meet classroom expectations because… *(describe specific work not done):*

The reasons why I was not prepared were:

List three ways you can avoid this problem in the future, then circle the best one:

1.

2.

3.

Being Prepared for Class

DIRECTIONS: Read the following paragraphs and be prepared to have a discussion with your teacher/administrator.

Everyone has jobs and responsibilities. As a student, my job is school. By not being prepared for class, I failed to take care of my responsibilities. If I am not prepared for class, the teacher has to spend valuable class time helping me get the materials I need. Sometimes this can be difficult, and it disrupts classmates. Other times, I earn an incomplete or a lower grade because I am not prepared. When doing group activities, not being prepared can slow the class and force others in my group to do more work. That is not fair to my peers. **On the other hand, being prepared for class can improve my grades and make class less stressful.**

When I'm older, the consequences can be more serious if I fail to meet my responsibilities. In college, students who are not prepared for their classes can fail. On the job, employees who are not prepared for their jobs can lose promotions or be fired. **However, individuals who prepare and take care of their responsibilities enjoy more success in school, at work, and at home.**

I understand my teacher is trying to help me learn how to be more responsible so I will have more success in school. It is my responsibility to fix this behavior. If I do not use the skill of **Being Prepared for Class,** I will earn additional consequences.

I will strive to do better in the future.

_____   _____
SIGNATURE   DATE

Being On Time for School or Class

DIRECTIONS: Read the following sentences carefully and answer by filling in the blanks or writing in the space provided. Please use complete sentences.

I broke a school/classroom rule when I… (describe when and where you were tardy):

The reasons why I have been late for school or class are:

List three ways you can avoid this problem in the future, then circle the best one:

1.

2.

3.

Being On Time for School or Class

DIRECTIONS: Read the following paragraphs and be prepared to have a discussion with your teacher/administrator.

Everyone has responsibilities. As a student, my responsibility is to get to school and class on time. When I'm tardy, I am not being responsible or dependable. When I show up late, I miss announcements and important information about assignments and activities. This can make me fall behind in my schoolwork and have to depend on others to share their notes with me. They may not always want to share, or their notes may be incomplete. This makes it harder to catch up and creates more work and stress for me. I also disrupt the teacher and distract my classmates when I walk in late. That is not fair to them. **On the other hand, being on time makes it easier for me to stay up to speed in my classes, and I don't feel rushed all the time. I also show more respect to my teachers and classmates.**

When I'm older, the consequences can be more serious if I fail to meet expectations by showing up late. Others will consider me unreliable and not trustworthy. I can lose friendships and damage my relationships with family members and coworkers. **However, when I'm on time, I feel better about myself and others see me as dependable.**

I understand my teacher is trying to help me learn how to meet expectations by being on time for school and class. It is my responsibility to fix this behavior. If I continue showing up late for school or class, I will earn additional consequences.

I will strive to do better in the future.

_____   _____

SIGNATURE   DATE

Showing Sensitivity to Others

DIRECTIONS: Read the following sentences carefully and answer by filling in the blanks or writing in the space provided. Please use complete sentences.

I did not show sensitivity when I… (describe your inappropriate words and/or actions):

The reasons for my insensitive behavior were:

List three ways you can avoid this problem in the future, then circle the best one:

1.

2.

3.

THINK SHEETS AND MEDIATION ESSAYS

The following blank Think Sheets and Mediation Essays are designed for the administrator/interventionist to choose any skill or behavior that a student may have encountered resulting in suspension. To use, the administrator/interventionist should identify the skill or behavior at the top of the sheet, then the student will answer or discuss the prompts on the Think Sheets and Mediation Essays. Any blanks the student encounters will need to be filled in with the skill from the first page.

SKILL:

Today, I...

Should have _____

_____

Should not have _____

_____

The skill of _____ is expected at my school. The student handbook mentions it in several places. There are many reasons why using this skill is an important rule at my school. Some of the reasons why I should use this skill include (list 3 to 4 reasons):

Using _____ at school is particularly important to me for two reasons (choose two from the list above):

(continued)

In the future, I will try to use the skill of _____.
The steps of the skill are:

Of the five skill steps previously listed, the three I need to improve on the most are:

If I need help _____, I will ask a
teacher, administrator, or counselor to help me. Or, I will ask a friend or talk to a family
member. **The people or resources I can use to help me are:**

At school, there are consequences for not _____.
Consequences can include correction from a teacher, detention, office referral, in-school
suspension, meeting with a teacher or administrator, and phone calls home. In addition,
there are natural consequences, including losing the respect of others, earning a bad
reputation, being embarrassed, straining relationships, and losing leadership
opportunities in class and extracurricular activities. **The consequences I want to
avoid are:**

(continued)

> **DIRECTIONS:** You may need to refer to the previous pages to answer the following questions. For each question, write a response using at least two complete sentences. If your answers are not written appropriately (capitalization, punctuation, and readable handwriting), you may have to redo the worksheet.

What are two reasons why you should use the skill of _____ at school and school-sponsored activities?

How are you hurt when you don't use _____ at school?

What two actions or steps do you plan to take to help you use the skill of _____ _____ at school?

There may be more negative consequences in the future if you _____ _____ at school. What are two possible consequences?

What are two benefits or good things that can happen when you use _____ _____ at school?

_____   _____
SIGNATURE   DATE

SKILL:

DIRECTIONS: Read the following sentences carefully and answer by filling in the blanks or writing in the space provided. Please use complete sentences.

I behaved inappropriately when I... (describe the situation, including who was involved and your behavior):

The reasons why I behaved inappropriately and _____ **were:**

List three ways you can avoid this problem in the future, then circle the best one:

1.

2.

3.

_____   _____
SIGNATURE   DATE

SKILL:

DIRECTIONS: Sit quietly and answer the following essay questions on a separate sheet of paper. Print or write neatly. When finished, raise your hand and be prepared to discuss the essay.

What did I do wrong?

What could happen to me?

Why was it wrong?

What should I do?

What good things will happen to me?

Index of Skills

THE FOLLOWING SECTION IS A LIST OF SKILLS AND SKILL STEPS THAT SHOULD BE USED DURING THE **PAS** PROCESS. Each chapter has common skills associated with the behavioral scenario as a guideline for skills to focus on for re-teaching. Not all of the skills need to be used for every situation. What skill(s) you teach to students is based on their individual needs and an explanation of the incident that resulted in the suspension. Boys Town also offers a great resource book, "Teaching Social Skills to Youth," that outlines more than 180 skills that are task analyzed with steps and broken into beginning, intermediate, advanced, and complex skills. The skills listed in this book are a great start but student needs are varied and "Teaching Social Skills to Youth" is an excellent resource that can help address other skills students may need.

✱ CHAPTER 1 SKILLS
Code of Conduct

Accepting criticism (feedback) or a consequence

1. Look at the person.
2. Say "Okay."
3. Don't argue.

Accepting decisions of authority

1. Look at the person.
2. Remain calm and monitor your feelings and behavior.
3. Use a pleasant or neutral tone of voice.
4. Acknowledge the decision by saying "Okay" or "Yes, I understand."
5. If you disagree, do so at a later time.
6. Refrain from arguing, pouting, or becoming angry.

Using an appropriate voice tone

1. Look at the person you are talking to.
2. Listen to the level and quality of the voice tone you are speaking with.
3. Lower your voice (if necessary) so that it isn't too loud or harsh.
4. Speak slowly. Think about what you want to say.
5. Concentrate on making your voice sound calm, neutral, or even pleasant and happy.
6. Avoid shouting, whining, or begging.

Doing good quality work

1. Find out the exact expectations or instructions for tasks.
2. Assemble the necessary tools or materials.
3. Carefully begin working. Focus your attention on the task.
4. Continue working until the task is completed or criteria are met.
5. Examine the results of your work to make sure it was done correctly.
6. Correct any deficiencies, if necessary. Perhaps, check back with the person who assigned the task.

Showing respect

1. Obey a request to stop a negative behavior.

2. Refrain from teasing, threatening, or making fun of others.

3. Allow others to have their privacy.

4. Obtain permission before using another person's property.

5. Do not damage or vandalize public property.

6. Refrain from conning or persuading others into breaking rules.

7. Avoid acting obnoxiously in public.

8. Dress appropriately when in public.

Following rules

1. Learn what rules apply to the current situation.

2. Adjust your behavior so you are following the rules exactly.

3. Refrain from "bending" rules, even just a little.

4. If you have questions, find the appropriate adult to ask about the rules in question.

✱ CHAPTER 2 SKILLS
Defiance, Non-Compliance, and Insubordination

Following instructions

1. Look at the person.

2. Say "Okay."

3. Do what you've been asked right away.

Complying with reasonable requests

1. Look at the person making the request.

2. Use a pleasant or neutral tone of voice.

3. Acknowledge the request by saying "Okay" or "Sure."

4. Promptly complete the requested activity.

5. If you are unable to do so, politely tell the person that you cannot do what he or she requested.

Disagreeing appropriately

1. Look at the person.
2. Use a pleasant voice.
3. Say "I understand how you feel."
4. Tell why you feel differently.
5. Give a reason.
6. Listen to the other person.

Accepting criticism (feedback) or a consequence

1. Look at the person.
2. Say "Okay."
3. Don't argue.

Making a request (Asking a favor)

1. Look at the person.
2. Use a clear, pleasant voice tone.
3. Make your request in the form of a question by saying "Would you…" and "Please…."
4. If your request is granted, remember to say "Thank you."
5. If your request is denied, remember to accept "No" for an answer.

✳ CHAPTER 3 SKILLS
Harassment / Boundaries

Controlling emotions

1. Learn what situations cause you to lose control or make you angry.

2. Monitor the feelings you have in stressful situations.

3. Instruct yourself to breathe deeply and relax when stressful feelings begin to arise.

4. Reword angry feelings so they can be expressed appropriately and calmly to others.

5. Praise yourself for controlling emotional outbursts.

Making a request (Asking a favor)

1. Look at the person.

2. Use a clear, pleasant voice tone.

3. Make your request in the form of a question by saying "Would you…" and "Please…."

4. If your request is granted, remember to say "Thank you."

5. If your request is denied, remember to accept "No" for an answer.

Accepting "No" for an answer

1. Look at the person.

2. Say "Okay."

3. Stay calm.

4. If you disagree, ask later.

Dealing with frustration

1. Identify feelings of frustration as they arise.

2. Determine the source of these feelings.

3. Breathe deeply and relax when frustrations arise.

4. Discuss frustrations with a caring adult or peer.

5. Find alternative activities that promote feelings of success.

Choosing appropriate words to say

1. Look at the situation and the people around you.
2. Know the meanings of words you are about to say.
3. Refrain from using words that will offend people around you or that they will not understand.
4. Avoid using slang, profanity, or words that could have a sexual meaning.
5. Decide what thought you want to put into words and then say the words.

Using an appropriate voice tone

1. Look at the person you are talking to.
2. Listen to the level and quality of the voice tone you are speaking with.
3. Lower your voice (if necessary) so that it isn't too loud or harsh.
4. Speak slowly. Think about what you want to say.
5. Concentrate on making your voice sound calm, neutral, or even pleasant and happy.
6. Avoid shouting, whining, or begging.

Following instructions

1. Look at the person.
2. Say "Okay."
3. Do what you've been asked right away.

Accepting criticism (feedback) or a consequence

1. Look at the person.
2. Say "Okay."
3. Don't argue.

Greeting others

1. Look at the person.
2. Use a pleasant voice.
3. Say "Hi" or "Hello."

Self-correcting own behaviors

1. Monitor your behaviors during difficult or stressful circumstances.
2. Notice the effects your behaviors have on other people. Notice their response to what you say.
3. Instruct yourself to correct behaviors that appear to make others uncomfortable.
4. Use new behaviors and note their effects.
5. Continue to make adjustments, as necessary.
6. Reward yourself for correcting your own behaviors.

Problem-solving a disagreement

1. Look at the person.
2. Remain calm. Use a pleasant voice.
3. Identify options for solving the disagreement.
4. Consider the potential consequences.
5. Choose the best solution for the situation.
6. Be open to the other person's views.

Compromising with others

1. Identify disagreements before they get out of hand.
2. Suggest alternative activities you and your peer could agree to do.
3. Listen to what your peer suggests.
4. Remain calm and continue to talk about a compromise.

Making an apology

1. Look at the person.
2. Use a serious, sincere voice tone, but don't pout.
3. Begin by saying "I wanted to apologize for..." or "I'm sorry for...."
4. Do not make excuses or try to rationalize your behavior.
5. Sincerely say you will try not to repeat the same behavior in the future.
6. Offer to compensate or pay restitution.
7. Thank the other person for listening.

✱ CHAPTER 4 SKILLS
Fighting

Cooperating with others

1. Discuss mutual goals or tasks with others.
2. Know what you must do to help accomplish those goals.
3. Give and accept constructive feedback appropriately with peers.
4. Follow rules if you are playing a game and share resources with others.
5. Praise peers' efforts and cooperation.

Coping with anger and aggression from others

1. Look at the person.
2. Remain calm and take deep breaths.
3. Use a neutral voice and facial expression; no laughing or smirking.
4. Avoid critical or sarcastic comments.
5. Listen to and acknowledge what the other person is saying.
6. If the other person becomes aggressive or abusive, leave the situation.
7. Report the incident to an adult.

Coping with conflict

1. Remain calm and relaxed.
2. Listen to what the people in conflict are saying.
3. Think of helpful options.
4. If appropriate, offer options to the people who are involved in the conflict.
5. If the situation becomes aggressive or dangerous, remove yourself.

Compromising with others

1. Identify disagreements before they get out of hand.
2. Suggest alternative activities you and your peer could agree to do.
3. Listen to what your peer suggests.
4. Remain calm and continue to talk about a compromise.

Accepting "No" for an answer

1. Look at the person.
2. Say "Okay."
3. Stay calm.
4. If you disagree, ask later.

Communicating honestly

1. Look at the person.
2. Use a clear voice. Avoid stammering or hesitating.
3. Respond to questions factually and completely.
4. Do not leave out details or important facts.
5. Truthfully take responsibility for any inappropriate behaviors you displayed.

Analyzing tasks to be completed

1. Clarify what task or assignment has been given to you.
2. List every step you need to do in order to complete the task.
3. Identify which step needs to be done first, second, third, etc.
4. Begin completing the steps in order.

Controlling emotions

1. Learn what situations cause you to lose control or make you angry.
2. Monitor the feelings you have in stressful situations.
3. Instruct yourself to breathe deeply and relax when stressful feelings begin to arise.
4. Reword angry feelings so they can be expressed appropriately and calmly to others.
5. Praise yourself for controlling emotional outbursts.

Making a request (Asking a favor)

1. Look at the person.
2. Use a clear, pleasant voice tone.
3. Make your request in the form of a question by saying "Would you..." and "Please...."
4. If your request is granted, remember to say "Thank you."
5. If your request is denied, remember to accept "No" for an answer.

Using anger control strategies

1. If a person is talking to you, continue listening and acknowledging what he or she is saying.
2. Monitor your body's feelings and how quickly you are breathing.
3. Breathe slowly and deeply.
4. Give yourself instructions to continue breathing deeply and relax your tense body areas.
5. If appropriate, calmly ask the other person for a few minutes to be by yourself.
6. While you are alone, continue to monitor your feelings and instruct yourself to relax.

Dealing with frustration

1. Identify feelings of frustration as they arise.
2. Determine the source of these feelings.
3. Breathe deeply and relax when frustrations arise.
4. Discuss frustrations with a caring adult or peer.
5. Find alternative activities that promote feelings of success.

Using an appropriate voice tone

1. Look at the person you are talking to.
2. Listen to the level and quality of the voice tone you are speaking with.
3. Lower your voice (if necessary) so that it isn't too loud or harsh.
4. Speak slowly. Think about what you want to say.
5. Concentrate on making your voice sound calm, neutral, or even pleasant and happy.
6. Avoid shouting, whining, or begging.

Following instructions

1. Look at the person.
2. Say "Okay."
3. Do what you've been asked right away.

Accepting criticism (feedback) or a consequence

1. Look at the person.
2. Say "Okay."
3. Don't argue.

Greeting others

1. Look at the person.
2. Use a pleasant voice.
3. Say "Hi" or "Hello."

✳ CHAPTER 5 SKILLS
Bullying/Threatening Others

Controlling emotions

1. Learn what situations cause you to lose control or make you angry.
2. Monitor the feelings you have in stressful situations.
3. Instruct yourself to breathe deeply and relax when stressful feelings begin to arise.
4. Reword angry feelings so they can be expressed appropriately and calmly to others.
5. Praise yourself for controlling emotional outbursts.

Making a request (Asking a favor)

1. Look at the person.
2. Use a clear, pleasant voice tone.
3. Make your request in the form of a question by saying "Would you..." and "Please...."
4. If your request is granted, remember to say "Thank you."
5. If your request is denied, remember to accept "No" for an answer.

Dealing with frustration

1. Identify feelings of frustration as they arise.
2. Determine the source of these feelings.
3. Breathe deeply and relax when frustrations arise.
4. Discuss frustrations with a caring adult or peer.
5. Find alternative activities that promote feelings of success.

Using anger control strategies

1. If a person is talking to you, continue listening and acknowledging what he or she is saying.
2. Monitor your body's feelings and how quickly you are breathing.
3. Breathe slowly and deeply.
4. Give yourself instructions to continue breathing deeply and relax your tense body areas.
5. If appropriate, calmly ask the other person for a few minutes to be by yourself.
6. While you are alone, continue to monitor your feelings and instruct yourself to relax.

Using an appropriate voice tone

1. Look at the person you are talking to.
2. Listen to the level and quality of the voice tone you are speaking with.
3. Lower your voice (if necessary) so that it isn't too loud or harsh.
4. Speak slowly. Think about what you want to say.
5. Concentrate on making your voice sound calm, neutral, or even pleasant and happy.
6. Avoid shouting, whining, or begging.

Following instructions

1. Look at the person.
2. Say "Okay."
3. Do what you've been asked right away.

Accepting criticism (feedback) or a consequence

1. Look at the person.
2. Say "Okay."
3. Don't argue.

Greeting others

1. Look at the person.
2. Use a pleasant voice.
3. Say "Hi" or "Hello."

Self-correcting own behaviors

1. Monitor your behaviors during difficult or stressful circumstances.
2. Notice the effects your behaviors have on other people. Notice their response to what you say.
3. Instruct yourself to correct behaviors that appear to make others uncomfortable.
4. Use new behaviors and note their effects.
5. Continue to make adjustments, as necessary.
6. Reward yourself for correcting your own behaviors.

Showing respect

1. Obey a request to stop a negative behavior.
2. Refrain from teasing, threatening, or making fun of others.
3. Allow others to have their privacy.
4. Obtain permission before using another person's property.
5. Do not damage or vandalize public property.
6. Refrain from conning or persuading others into breaking rules.
7. Avoid acting obnoxiously in public.
8. Dress appropriately when in public.

Problem-solving a disagreement

1. Look at the person.
2. Remain calm. Use a pleasant voice.
3. Identify options for solving the disagreement.
4. Consider the potential consequences.
5. Choose the best solution for the situation.
6. Be open to the other person's views.

Compromising with others

1. Identify disagreements before they get out of hand.
2. Suggest alternative activities you and your peer could agree to do.
3. Listen to what your peer suggests.
4. Remain calm and continue to talk about a compromise.

Making an apology

1. Look at the person.
2. Use a serious, sincere voice tone, but don't pout.
3. Begin by saying "I wanted to apologize for..." or "I'm sorry for...."
4. Do not make excuses or try to rationalize your behavior.
5. Sincerely say you will try not to repeat the same behavior in the future.
6. Offer to compensate or pay restitution.
7. Thank the other person for listening.

✱ CHAPTER 6 SKILLS
Aggression toward Property

Accepting criticism (feedback) or a consequence

1. Look at the person.
2. Say "Okay."
3. Don't argue.

Disagreeing appropriately

1. Look at the person.
2. Use a pleasant voice.
3. Say "I understand how you feel."
4. Tell why you feel differently.
5. Give a reason.
6. Listen to the other person.

Showing respect

1. Obey a request to stop a negative behavior.
2. Refrain from teasing, threatening, or making fun of others.
3. Allow others to have their privacy.
4. Obtain permission before using another person's property.
5. Do not damage or vandalize public property.
6. Refrain from conning or persuading others into breaking rules.
7. Avoid acting obnoxiously in public.
8. Dress appropriately when in public.

Accepting decisions of authority

1. Look at the person.
2. Remain calm and monitor your feelings and behavior.
3. Use a pleasant or neutral tone of voice.
4. Acknowledge the decision by saying "Okay" or "Yes, I understand."
5. If you disagree, do so at a later time.
6. Refrain from arguing, pouting, or becoming angry.

Making an apology

1. Look at the person.
2. Use a serious, sincere voice tone, but don't pout.
3. Begin by saying "I wanted to apologize for..." or "I'm sorry for...."
4. Do not make excuses or try to rationalize your behavior.
5. Sincerely say you will try not to repeat the same behavior in the future.
6. Offer to compensate or pay restitution.
7. Thank the other person for listening.

Using anger control strategies

1. If a person is talking to you, continue listening and acknowledging what he or she is saying.
2. Monitor your body's feelings and how quickly you are breathing.
3. Breathe slowly and deeply.
4. Give yourself instructions to continue breathing deeply and relax your tense body areas.
5. If appropriate, calmly ask the other person for a few minutes to be by yourself.
6. While you are alone, continue to monitor your feelings and instruct yourself to relax.

Making restitution (Compensating)

1. Begin by making an appropriate apology.
2. Offer to compensate for any offenses you may have committed.
3. Follow through on restitution promises.
4. Thank the person for allowing you to make compensation.

Dealing with frustration

1. Identify feelings of frustration as they arise.
2. Determine the source of these feelings.
3. Breathe deeply and relax when frustrations arise.
4. Discuss frustrations with a caring adult or peer.
5. Find alternative activities that promote feelings of success.

✳ CHAPTER 7 SKILLS
Impulse Control

Following instructions

1. Look at the person.
2. Say "Okay."
3. Do what you've been asked right away.

Accepting criticism (feedback) or a consequence

1. Look at the person.
2. Say "Okay."
3. Don't argue.

Concentrating on a subject or task

1. Promptly begin work on a task.
2. Focus your attention directly on the subject.
3. If your attention wanders, instruct yourself to concentrate on the task.
4. Ignore distractions or interruptions by others.
5. Remain on task until the work is completed.

Displaying effort

1. Remain on task and work diligently.
2. Do your best to accomplish tasks to criteria.
3. Inform others of your efforts, if appropriate.

Completing tasks

1. Listen carefully to instructions or directions for tasks.
2. Assemble the necessary tools or materials needed for the task.
3. Begin working carefully and neatly.
4. Remain focused on the task until it is completed.
5. Examine the product of your work to make sure it is complete.
6. Check back with the person who assigned the task.

Controlling emotions

1. Learn what situations cause you to lose control or make you angry.
2. Monitor the feelings you have in stressful situations.
3. Instruct yourself to breathe deeply and relax when stressful feelings begin to arise.
4. Reword angry feelings so they can be expressed appropriately and calmly to others.
5. Praise yourself for controlling emotional outbursts.

Choosing appropriate words to say

1. Look at the situation and the people around you.
2. Know the meanings of words you are about to say.
3. Refrain from using words that will offend people around you or that they will not understand.
4. Avoid using slang, profanity, or words that could have a sexual meaning.
5. Decide what thought you want to put into words and then say the words.

Complying with reasonable requests

1. Look at the person making the request.
2. Use a pleasant or neutral tone of voice.
3. Acknowledge the request by saying "Okay" or "Sure."
4. Promptly complete the requested activity.
5. If you are unable to do so, politely tell the person that you cannot do what he or she requested.

Showing respect

1. Obey a request to stop a negative behavior.
2. Refrain from teasing, threatening, or making fun of others.
3. Allow others to have their privacy.
4. Obtain permission before using another person's property.
5. Do not damage or vandalize public property.
6. Refrain from conning or persuading others into breaking rules.
7. Avoid acting obnoxiously in public.
8. Dress appropriately when in public.

Following rules

1. Learn what rules apply to the current situation.

2. Adjust your behavior so you are following the rules exactly.

3. Refrain from "bending" rules, even just a little.

4. If you have questions, find the appropriate adult to ask about the rules in question.

✳ CHAPTER 8 SKILLS
Stealing/Dishonesty

Controlling the impulse to steal

1. Identify and avoid situations in which you are likely to steal.

2. Before you steal, stop your behaviors immediately.

3. Instruct yourself to leave the area without stealing.

4. Consider the long-term consequences of stealing.

5. Self-report any previous stealing.

Making decisions

1. Accurately identify what decision you must make.

2. Examine what your choices currently appear to be.

3. Generate other choices, if possible.

4. Look at the potential consequences (positive and negative) of each choice.

5. Pick the first- and second-best choices based on the potential outcomes.

Making an apology

1. Look at the person.

2. Use a serious, sincere voice tone, but don't pout.

3. Begin by saying "I wanted to apologize for..." or "I'm sorry for...."

4. Do not make excuses or try to rationalize your behavior.

5. Sincerely say you will try not to repeat the same behavior in the future.

6. Offer to compensate or pay restitution.

7. Thank the other person for listening.

Dealing with an accusation

1. Look at the person with a neutral facial expression.
2. Remain calm and monitor your feelings and behavior.
3. Listen carefully to what the other person is saying.
4. Acknowledge what the person is saying or that a problem exists.
5. Ask if this is the appropriate time to respond. Say "May I respond to what you are saying?"
6. If the person says "Yes," respond truthfully and factually by either self-reporting, peer reporting, or honestly denying the accusation.

Making restitution (Compensating)

1. Begin by making an appropriate apology.
2. Offer to compensate for any offenses you may have committed.
3. Follow through on restitution promises.
4. Thank the person for allowing you to make compensation.

Borrowing from others

1. Appropriately ask to borrow something from another person.
2. Accept "No" if the person declines.
3. If the person agrees, find out when you need to return the possession you are borrowing.
4. Care for others' property while you have it and promptly return it when you are finished.

✳ CHAPTER 9 SKILLS
Weapons/Contraband/Drugs

Controlling the impulse to lie

1. Identify untrue statements before you say them.
2. Stop talking and pause.
3. Answer all questions factually and make only truthful statements.
4. Consider the long-term consequences of lying to others.
5. Apologize for any untrue statements you previously made.

Refraining from possessing contraband or drugs

1. Refuse to accept drugs or contraband from strangers, acquaintances, or peers.
2. Examine your own possessions and decide whether they are appropriate to have (legally, morally, rightfully yours).
3. Turn in drugs or contraband to an appropriate adult or authority figure.
4. Self-report your involvement; peer report, if necessary.
5. Honestly answer any questions that are asked.

Following safety rules

1. Learn the rules that apply to different situations.
2. Adjust behaviors according to directives in rules.
3. Do not "bend" or test safety rules.
4. Report others who break safety rules, for their own good.

Preventing trouble with others

1. Identify situations that commonly result in conflicts.
2. Review the skills necessary to handle those specific situations.
3. Approach situations with a positive voice, a smile, and a willingness to compromise.
4. Ask for advice from a caring adult.

Resisting peer pressure

1. Look at the person.

2. Use a calm, assertive voice tone.

3. State clearly that you do not want to engage in the inappropriate activity.

4. Suggest an alternative activity. Give a reason.

5. If the person persists, continue to say "No."

6. If the peer will not accept your "No" answer,
   ask him or her to leave or remove yourself from the situation.

Choosing appropriate friends

1. Think of the qualities and interests you would look for in a friend.

2. Look at the strengths and weaknesses of potential friends.

3. Match the characteristics of potential friends with activities and interests you would share.

4. Avoid peers who are involved with drugs, gangs, or breaking the law.

Communicating honestly

1. Look at the person.

2. Use a clear voice. Avoid stammering or hesitating.

3. Respond to questions factually and completely.

4. Do not leave out details or important facts.

5. Truthfully take responsibility for any inappropriate behaviors you displayed.

Dealing with group pressure

1. Look at the group.

2. Remain calm, but serious.

3. Assertively say "No" to inappropriate group activities.

4. If possible, suggest an alternative activity.

5. Remove yourself if pressure continues.

Keeping property in its place

1. Know where property is usually kept or belongs.

2. Ask the appropriate person for permission to remove property.

3. Take care of property you are responsible for.

4. Return the property to its place in its original condition.

Making decisions

1. Accurately identify what decision you must make.
2. Examine what your choices currently appear to be.
3. Generate other choices, if possible.
4. Look at the potential consequences (positive and negative) of each choice.
5. Pick the first- and second-best choices based on the potential outcomes.

Making restitution (Compensating)

1. Begin by making an appropriate apology.
2. Offer to compensate for any offenses you may have committed.
3. Follow through on restitution promises.
4. Thank the person for allowing you to make compensation.

Self-reporting own behaviors

1. Find the appropriate person to report to.
2. Look at the person.
3. Remain calm and use a neutral voice tone.
4. Truthfully and completely describe the behaviors you are reporting.
5. Honestly answer questions that are asked.
6. Peer report, if necessary.
7. Avoid making excuses or rationalizing behaviors.

Being an appropriate role model

1. Identify a situation requiring you to appropriately model behavior for younger peers or siblings.
2. Engage in positive interactions with adults or peers. Initiate only appropriate conversation topics.
3. Refrain from inappropriate language, sexual behavior, delinquency, bullying, etc.
4. Correct peer behavior in a positive, constructive manner.
5. Remember that inappropriate role-modeling can negatively affect younger children.

BIBLIOGRAPHY

American Psychological Association Zero Tolerance Task Force. (2008). Are zero tolerance policies effective in the schools?: An evidentiary review and recommendations. *The American Psychologist, 63*(9), 852-862. doi:1037/0003-066X.63.9.852

Bear, G. G., Yang, C., Pell, M., & Gaskins, C. (2014). Validation of a brief measure of teachers' perceptions of school climate: Relations to student achievement and suspensions. *Learning Environments Research, 17*(3), 339-354.

Cole, H. A., & Heilig, J. V. (2011). Developing a school-based youth court: A potential alternative to the school to prison pipeline. *Journal of Law and Education, 40*(2), 305.

Cornell, D. G., Gregory, A., & Fan, X. (2011). Reductions in long-term suspensions following adoption of the Virginia student threat assessment guidelines. *NASSP Bulletin, 95*(3), 175-194.

Davis-Ganao, J.S., Silvestre, F. S., & Glenn, J. W. (2013). Assessing the differential impact of contextual factors on school suspension for black and white students. *The Journal of Negro Education, 82*(4), 393-407.

Dickinson, M. C., & Miller, T. L. (2006). Issues regarding in-school suspensions and high school students with disabilities. *American Secondary Education, 35*(1), 72-83.

Dupper, D. R., Theriot, M. T., & Craun, S. W. (2009). Reducing out-of-school suspensions: Practice guidelines for school social workers. *Children & Schools [H.W. Wilson - EDUC], 31*(1), 6.

Freeman, S. M. (2007). Upholding students' due process rights: Why students are in need of better representation at, and alternatives to, school suspension hearings. *Family Court Review, 45*(4), 638-656.

Goran, L. G., & Gage, N. A. (2011). A comparative analysis of language, suspension, and academic performance of students with emotional disturbance and students with learning disabilities. *Education and Treatment of Children, 34*(4), 469-488.

Hannon, L., DeFina, R., & Bruch, S. (2013). The relationship between skin tone and school suspension for African Americans. *Race and Social Problems, 5*(4), 281.

Hemphill, S. A., Kotevski, A., Herrenkohl, T. I., Smith, R., Toumbourou, J. W., & Catalano, R. F. (2013). Does school suspension affect subsequent youth nonviolent antisocial behavior? A longitudinal study of students in Victoria, Australia and Washington state, United States. *Australian Journal of Psychology, 65*(4), 236-249.

Kiriakidis, P.P. & Robinson, C. (2014). Alternatives to suspending African American high school males. *Postmodern Openings,* (4), 145-155.

Krezmien, M. P., Leone, P. E., & Achilles, G. M. (2006). Suspension, race, and disability: Analysis of statewide practices and reporting. *Journal of Emotional and Behavioral Disorders, 14*(4), 217-226.

Lee, T., Cornell, D., Gregory, A., & Fan, X. (2011). High suspension schools and dropout rates for black and white students. *Education and Treatment of Children, 34*(2), 167-192. doi:10.1353/etc.2011.0014

Martinez, S. (2009). A system gone berserk: How are zero-tolerance policies really affecting schools? Preventing School Failure: *Alternative Education for Children and Youth, 53*(3), 153-158.

Noltemeyer, A. L., Ward, R. M., & Mcloughlin, C. (2015). Relationship between school suspension and student outcomes: A meta-analysis. *School Psychology Review, 44*(2), 224.

Perry, B. L., & Morris, E. W. (2014). Suspending progress: Collateral consequences of exclusionary punishment in public schools. *American Sociological Review, 79*(6), 1067-1087.

Schuck, P. H., Matera, M., & Noah, D. I. (2012). What happens to the "bad apples": An empirical study of suspensions in New York city schools. *Notre Dame Law Review, 87*(5), 2063.

Skiba, R. J. (2013). Reaching a critical juncture for our kids: The need to reassess school-justice practices. *Family Court Review, 51*(3), 380-387.

Smith, R. Y. (2015). A review of prelude to prison: Student perspectives on school suspension. *Journal of Pan African Studies, 8*(3), 136.

Stone, D. H., & Stone, L. S. (2011). Dangerous & disruptive or simply cutting class; when should schools kick kids to the curb? An empirical study of school suspension and due process rights. *Journal of Law & Family Studies, 13*(1), 1.

Teasley, M. L., & Miller, C. R. (2011). School social workers' perceived efficacy at tasks related to curbing suspension and undesirable behaviors. *Children & Schools, 33*(3), 136-145.

Teske, S. C. (2011). A study of zero tolerance policies in schools: A multi-integrated systems approach to improve outcomes for adolescents. *Journal of Child and Adolescent Psychiatric Nursing, 24*(2), 88-97.

REFERENCES

American Academy of Pediatrics. Council on School health. (2013). Policy statement: Out-of-school suspension and expulsion. *Pediatrics, 131,* 1000-1007.

American Academy of Pediatrics (2003). Out of school suspension and expulsion. *Pediatrics, 112*(5), 1206-1209.

Bellini, S. (2006). *Building social relationships: A systematic approach to teaching social interaction skills to children and adolescents with autism spectrum disorders and other social difficulties.* Shawnee Mission, KS: Autism Asperger Publishing Co.

Gresham, F.M. (1998). Social skills training: Should we raze, remodel, or rebuild? *Behavioral Disorders, 24*(1), 19-25.

Tierney, J., Green, E., & Dowd, T. (2016). *Teaching social skills to youth: An easy-to-follow guide to teaching 183 basic to complex life skills,* (3rd ed.). Boys Town, NE: Boys Town Press.

Peterson, R.L. (2005). Ten alternatives to suspension. *Impact, 18* (2), 10-11.

Pratt, D., Dillon, J.C., & Odermann Mougey, M. (2010). *School administrator's resource guide.* Boys Town, NE: Boys Town Press.

ABOUT THE AUTHORS

CATHERINE DESALVO, MS, was principal at Boys Town's middle school for 20 years and collaborated on the development of the Positive Alternatives to Suspension (PAS) program for Boys Town. In her 40-year career in education, she has been a teacher, behavioral consultant, and principal. She truly believes what Father Flanagan said: "There are no bad boys [or girls]. There is only bad environment, bad training, bad example, and bad thinking." She is confident students and schools will benefit from the PAS approach. Currently, she is the Supervisor of Multi-Tiered Systems of Support-Behavior for the Omaha Public Schools.

MIKE MEEKS, MS, is the National Training Manager for Boys Town's National Training Department. He has a B.S. In Elementary Education, M.S. in Human Services Administration, co-authored *Specialized Classroom Management* and *Well-Managed Schools, 2nd ed.*, and has written numerous curricula involving students and behavior. In his 15 years at Boys Town, he has worked with many students with behavioral difficulties, processed thousands of office referrals, and has used this knowledge and experience to train and consult to hundreds of schools and organizations across the country on systems to address student behavior.

DR. MATTHEW BUCKMAN received his doctorate from the University of Kentucky and received specialized training in Behavioral Pediatrics at the Boys Town Center for Behavioral Health. Currently, he is the Clinical Director of the Child & Adolescent Division at Egyptian Public & Mental Health Department where he supervises and provides direct services to children, teens, and families for a variety of emotional and behavioral health issues. Dr. Buckman also provides supervision, consultation, and training within various organizations and programs throughout southern Illinois, including educational, medical, and clinical settings.